Building Thinking Skills®

BEGINNING

Question and Answer Puzzles to Improve Academic Performance

SERIES TITLES
Building Thinking Skills®
Beginning • Primary • Level 1
Level 2 • Level 3 Figural • Level 3 Verbal

Written By
Michael O. Baker
Stephanie Stevens

Graphic Design By
Karla Garrett
Anna Allshouse

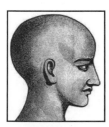

© 2008
THE CRITICAL THINKING CO.™
(Bright Minds™)
www.CriticalThinking.com
Phone: 800-458-4849 • Fax: 831-393-3277
P.O. Box 1610 • Seaside • CA 93955-1610
ISBN 978-0-89455-911-2

TABLE OF CONTENTS

SKILLS

Visual Tracking	3,7,11,12,19,23,32,38,47,52,56,70,71,75,82,83,85,93,96,97,109,111,112,115,122,124, 126,135,159,167,173,177,179,180,183,187,188,193,208
Visual Constancy	11,14,19,24,27,32,36,37,42,43,44,47,52,58,60,63,70,71,73,74,77,78,79,81,82,85,87, 88,89,95,99,103,104,108,109,113,116,121,123,125,127,132,134,136,140,154, 176,179,180,183,184,187,188,190,192,193,199,208,213
Visual Motor Skills	3,7,11,12,19,23,32,38,47,52,56,70,71,75,82,83,85,93,96,97,109,111,112,115,122,124, 126,159,167,173,177,180,183,187,188,190,193,208
Spatial Relationships	21,49,57,65,68,69,80,91,102,103,118,119,125,132,134,146,147,148,149,150,151, 154,155,156,157,161,162,163,164,175,178,183,184,187,189,190,194
Auditory Processing	* Every activity in this book requires the student to process auditory instructions. Many activities in this book require students to process one or more clues to produce a solution.
Auditory Memory	15,25,26,28,31,34,35,41,45,62,65,66,67,68,69,80,83,91,92,100,102,113,114,116,118, 119,120,128,149,153,160,161,165,166,169,170,171,172,174,175,178,186,189,213
Fine Motor Skill Development	3,7,11,12,19,23,24,37,38,47,52,70,71,75,82,83,85,93,96,97,109,111,112,115,122,124, 126,159,167,173,177,180,183,187,188,190,193,208
Inferential Reasoning/ Prediction	57,62,125,129,132,133,134,135,136,137,152,154,176,180,191,192,196,197,198, 200,201,202,203,204,205,206,209,210,212,214,215
Deduction	112,120,124,126,128,149,161,165,178,183,186,211
Identifying Similarities & Differences	1,2,3,4,5,6,8,9,14,16,17,18,20,22,27,29,30,36,41,42,43,44,48,50,51,53,55,60,61, 63,64,65,73,74,76,78,79,81,83,86,87,88,89,90,93,95,96,98,99,101,102,104,105, 106,108,110,112,113,115,116,117,121,123,124,126,127,132,134,135,136,140, 164,169,170,171,172,174,176,179,182,188,192,195,199,207
Classifying	10,24,27,37,41,42,50,51,52,53,59,60,71,81,85,88,89,97,99,104,107,109,112,113, 114,121,123,124,126,127,132,134,135,136,142,146,147,148,150,151,154,159, 164,184,188,196,197,198,200,201,202,203,204,205,206,207,209,210,212,214, 215,216,217,218
Identifying Sequences	13,39,77,94,103,129,133,137,152,153,179,180,181,182,190,191,192
Completing Analogies	196,197,198,200,201,202,203,204,205,206,209,210,212,214,215
Creative Problem Solving	145,173,177,187,193,208

CONCEPTS

Colors		
	Red	1,2,3,4,9,10,12,13,14,15,18,21,22,24,26,33,35,36,37,38,39,46,49,52,64,65,67,69,71,75, 77,78,79,80,83,84,86,87,90,91,94,96,98,99,100,101,103,105,113,138,139,141,142,144, 155,156,157,160,162,168,174,181,182,185,189,194
	Blue	5,6,7,8,9,10,11,12,13,14,15,21,22,24,26,28,31,33,36,37,39,40,46,49,54,56,59,65,68,69, 71,72,77,78,79,80,83,84,86,87,90,91,94,98,99,100,101,103,105,113,114,118,122,131, 138,139,142,143,144,155,157,162,168,174,194,195,213
	Yellow	16,17,18,19,20,21,22,23,24,26,28,33,34,36,37,39,40,46,49,54,59,64,65,67,69,77,78,79, 80,84,86,87,90,91,94,99,100,101,103,105,107,110,113,119,122,138,139,156,157,160, 162,168,175
	Green	29,30,31,32,33,35,36,37,38,39,40,46,52,54,64,65,67,69,72,75,77,78,79,80,86,87,90,91, 94,96,99,100,101,103,105,107,110,113,117,118,119,138,139,142,143,156,157,162,174, 175,181,182,189,195
Logical Connectives		
	And	26,40,72,84,98,110,117
	Or	26,40,72,84,98,110,117,166
Lines		
	Straight	44,45,46,47,48,49,51,52,54,55,56,59,61,67,71,81,85,106,131,163,166,175,182,194,195
	Curved	44,45,46,47,48,49,51,52,54,55,59,61,69,71,80,81,85,102,106,131,163,166,174,182,195
	Straight & Curved	48,51,52,55,56,59,61,81,131,158,163,195
Corners		63,64,65,67,69,70,72,75,80,92,106,158,185,213
Geometric Shapes		
	Circle	76,77,78,79,84,85,86,87,90,91,94,96,97,101,103,105,118,150,155,157,158,162,168,174, 176,211
	Triangle	86,87,90,91,92,94,95,96,97,101,102,103,105,114,125,131,145,150,151,156,157,160, 162,166,176,211
	Rectangle	99,100,101,102,103,105,106,107,109,110,113,115,116,117,118,119,120,122,125,141, 142,143,144,145,150,151,155,156,157,158,160,162,174,175,176,185,189,211
	Square	113,114,115,116,117,118,119,120,122,145,150,151,156,158,162,174,175,176,211
Behind & In-Between		130,131,164,178,185
Above & Below		92,161
Measurement		
	Longer	139,141
	Longest	139,141,143,144
	Shorter	138,141
	Shortest	138,141,143,144,175
	Larger	164
	Largest	168,169,170,171,172,185
	Smaller	164,168,169,170,171,172
	Smallest	168,169,170,171,172,174,185
Half & Whole		146,147,148,149,150,151,153,154,166,167,180,184,209
Left & Right		155,156,157,158,160,162,163,165,188
Open & Closed Figures		187,194

About This Book

Purpose: Young children often prefer to guess at an answer rather than apply an organized, analytical method to identify the solution. These activities develop organized analysis and critical thinking skills necessary for success in reading, writing, math, and science. They teach children the effectiveness of organized analysis and the joy (stimulation) in problem-solving.

Building Confidence and Improving Self-Esteem: Praise children's success with every clue and encourage them to finish these challenging puzzles. My favorite expression to use with young children who correctly identify a clue or answer is "You are so smart." This type of organized analysis is new to most children, so try to instill the confidence and determination to apply this type of reasoning to other aspects of education and life. Help them identify themselves as skilled problem-solvers.

Enrichment: Some of the activity types (unique problems, but same activity types) found in this book are available in other series we publish. For example, many children enjoy "Can You Find Me?" puzzles and "Clues & Choose" puzzles. We identify many of these activities in the book so you can identify the activity type and series.

We also offer a powerful preschool math program in our *Mathematical Reasoning*™ series and a powerful reading program in our *Mind Building Reading* series.

Teaching Suggestions

Note: Most 3-year-olds and 4-year-olds can do many of these activities with support from a teacher or parent; however, if a student struggles, don't be alarmed and jump to conclusions about the child's intelligence. Children's brains develop at different rates—especially young children. It is also common for individual students to grasp some concepts and struggle with others. If a student continues to struggle with a concept after your intervention, just move on to the next concept and try to come back a few days or weeks later.

Keep it Fun: Keep learning fun to avoid frustrating young children. Work around a child's attention span. Parents, please note that you have a great advantage to teach young children because most young children love to spend time with their moms and dads. If you keep learning fun, you will have an energetic pupil who looks forward to each and every lesson. Teachers, these activities can be done with small groups or individually.

Hands-On or Paper Activities: Many activities in the book can be taught "hands-on" with plastic geometric shapes or on paper using the pages in this book. The choice is yours and should depend on the needs of the student. Hands-on lessons can be especially helpful when a child struggles with a concept, however, there is no one "correct" way to teach the skills taught in this book. Use whatever method works best for each student.

Focus Paper: Young children often have trouble focusing on an activity—especially when there are other colorful objects on the page. A helpful tool to help them focus on the target is to use a blank piece of paper to cover the distractions (other activities) on the page.

Identifying Colors

This figure is colored red.

Point to the red figure in each row.

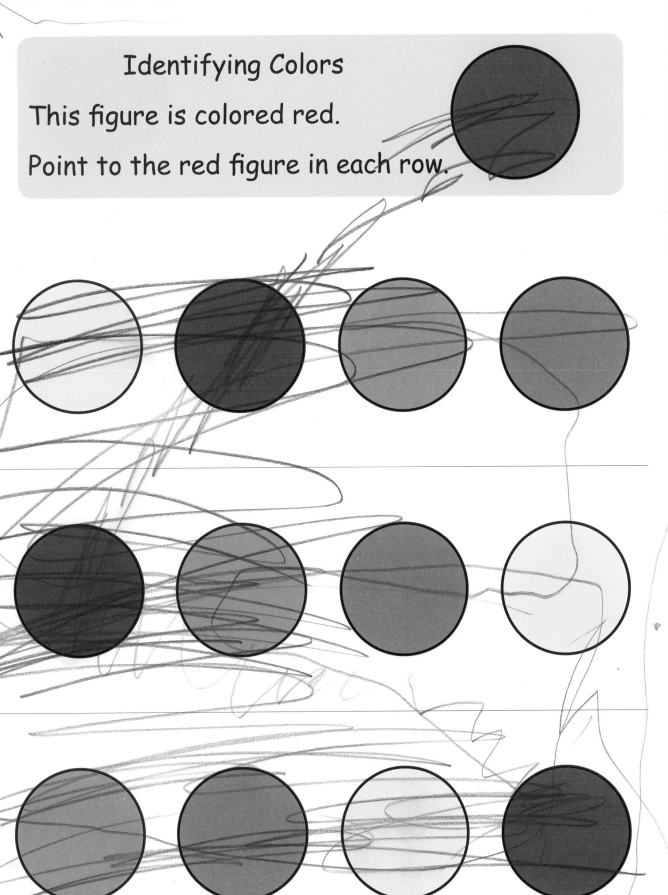

Identifying Colors

This figure is colored red.

Point to the red figure in each row.

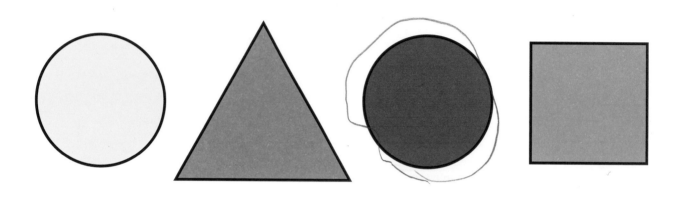

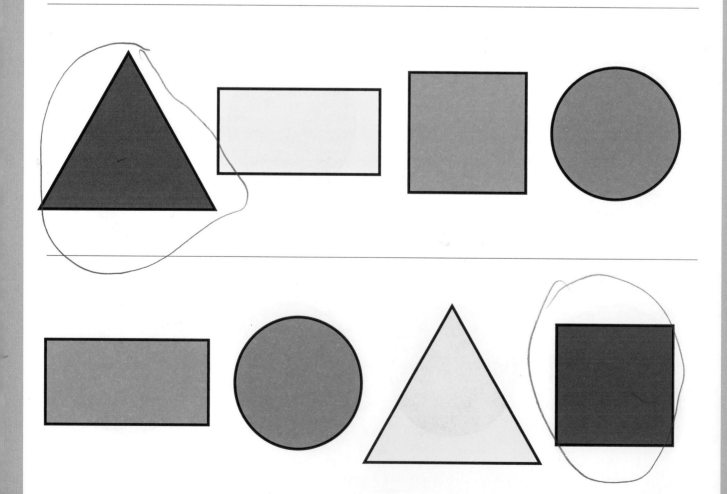

Draw one line connecting each red figure without touching any other color.

Start here.

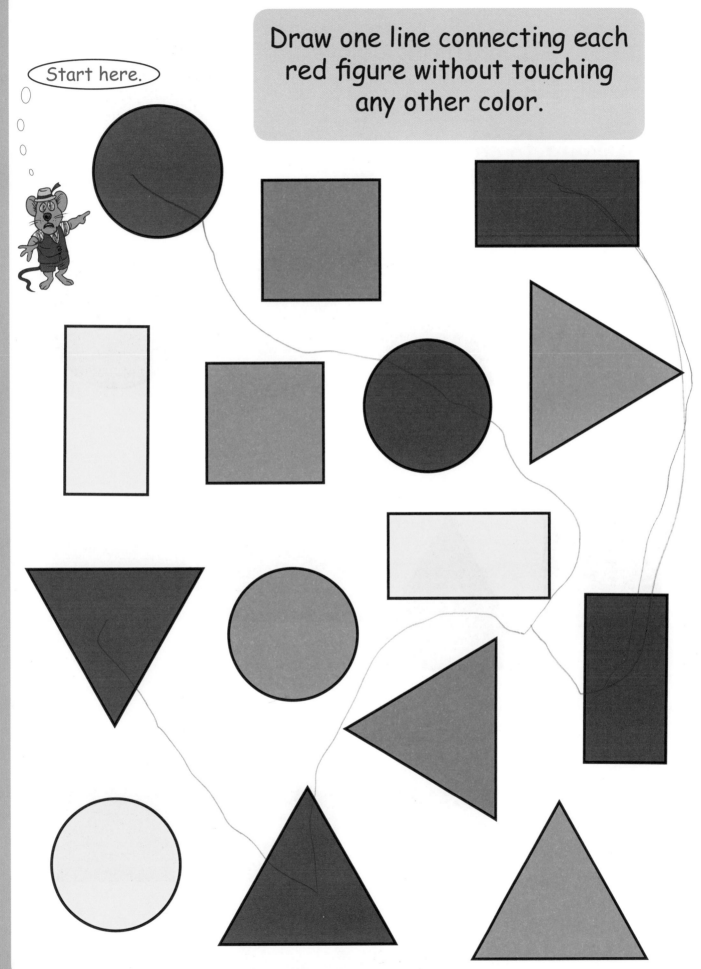

Identifying Colors

This figure is colored red.

Point to each red figure.

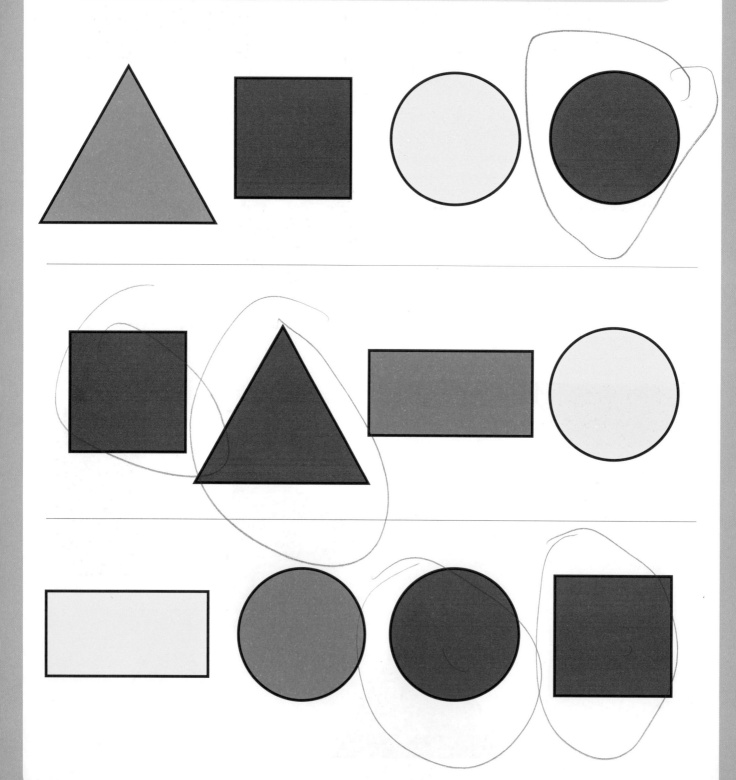

Identifying Colors

This figure is colored blue.

Point to the blue figure in each row.

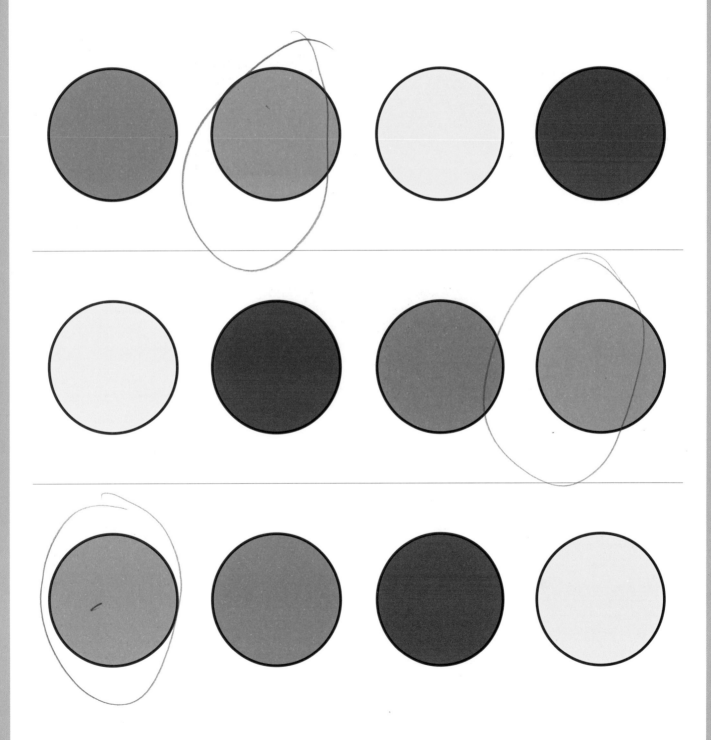

Identifying Colors

This figure is colored blue.

Point to the blue figure in each row.

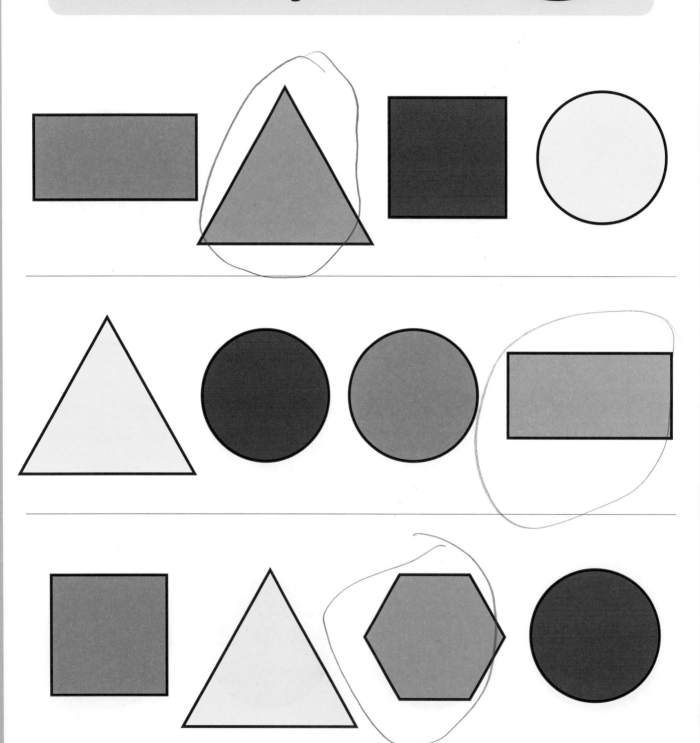

Start here.

Draw a line connecting each blue figure without touching any other color.

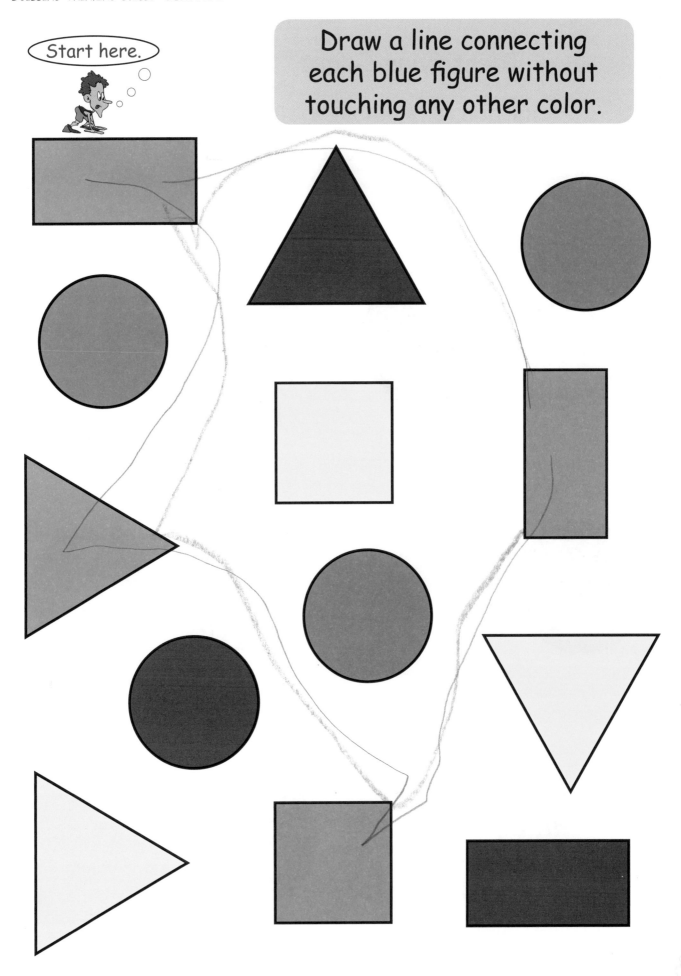

Identifying Colors

This figure is colored blue.

Point to each blue figure.

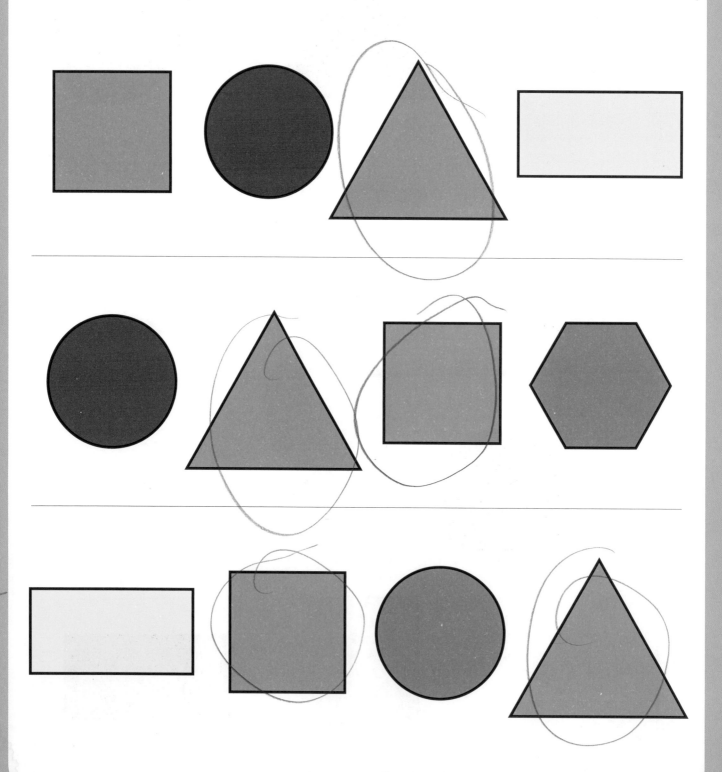

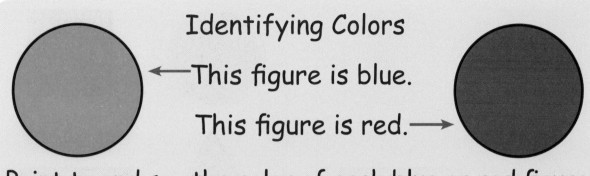

Identifying Colors

← This figure is blue.

This figure is red. →

Point to and say the color of each blue or red figure.

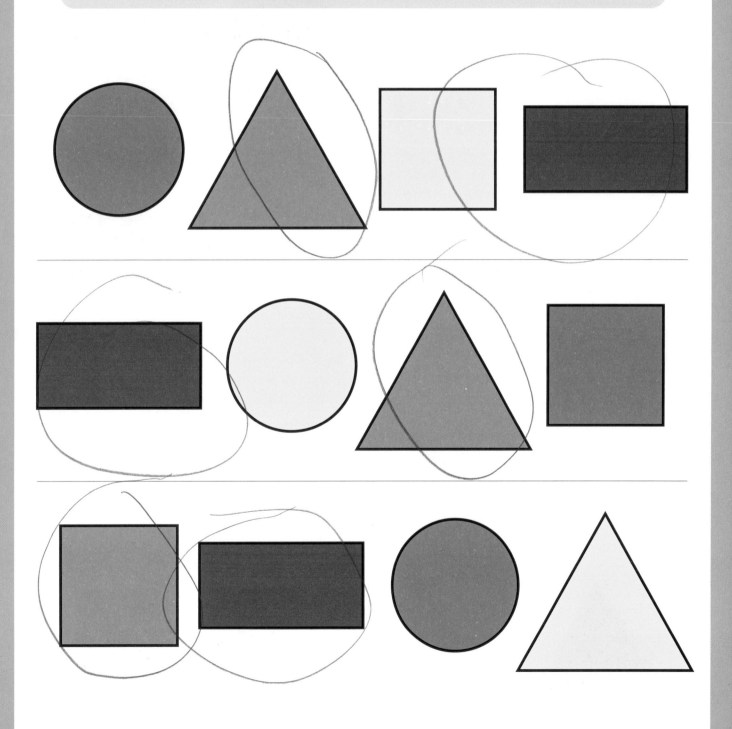

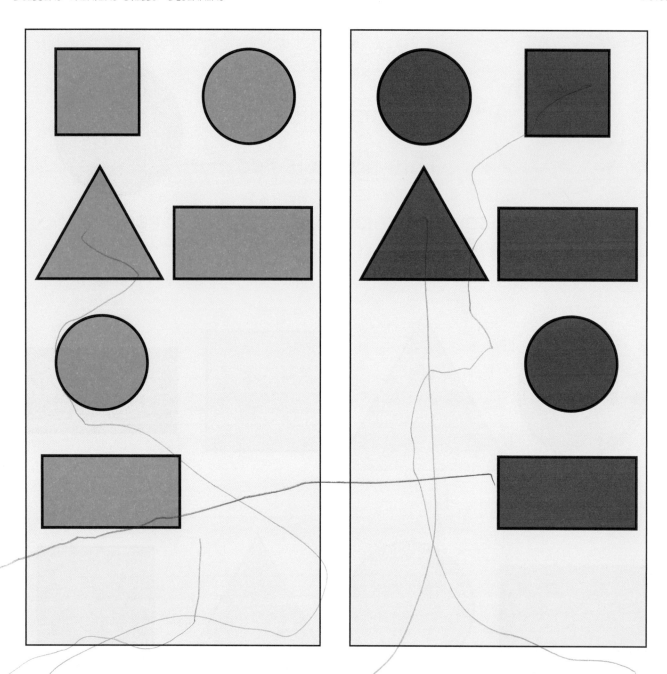

In which box does each figure below belong?
Draw a line from each figure to its box.

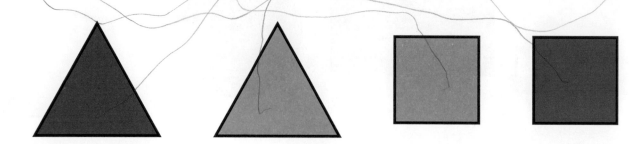

Start here.

Draw a line connecting each blue figure without touching any other color.

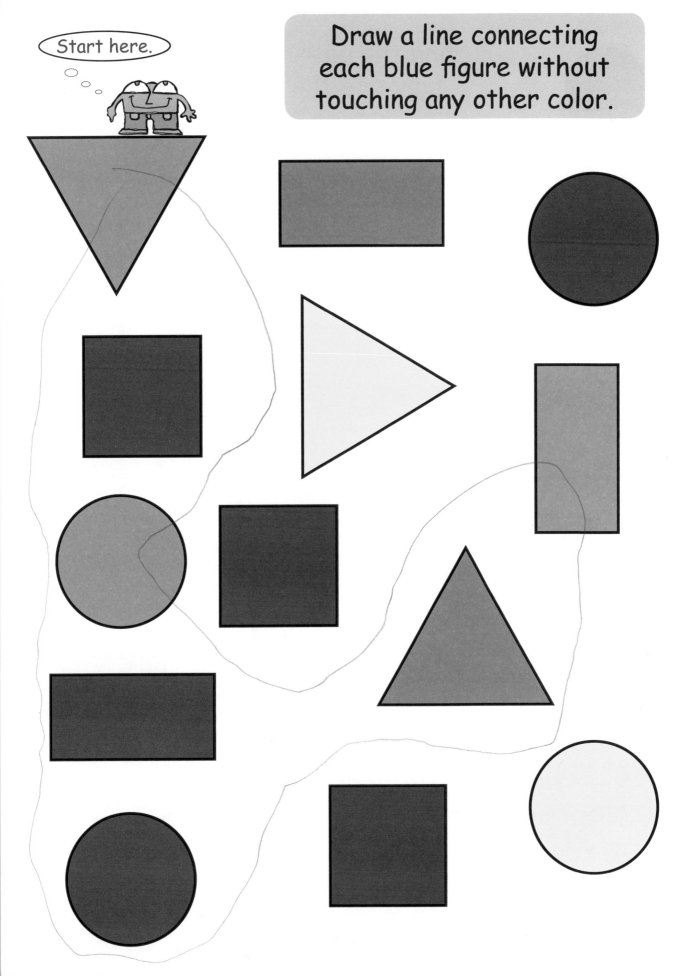

Find the path from the red figure to the blue figure.

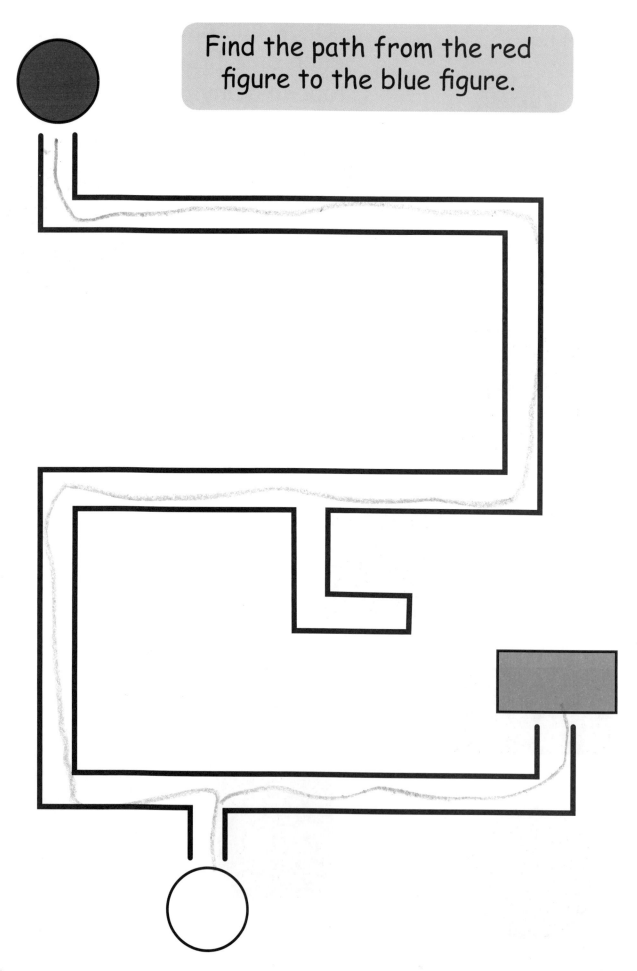

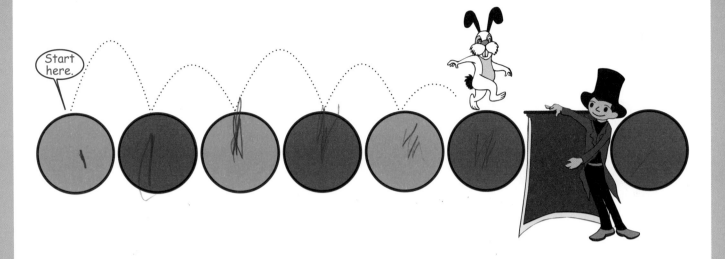

Say the color of each rabbit jump.
What color is the boy hiding?

Say the color of each scoop of ice cream.
What color is the girl hiding?

These two are red.

In each group there are two figures that are similar. Point to the two figures and tell why they are similar.

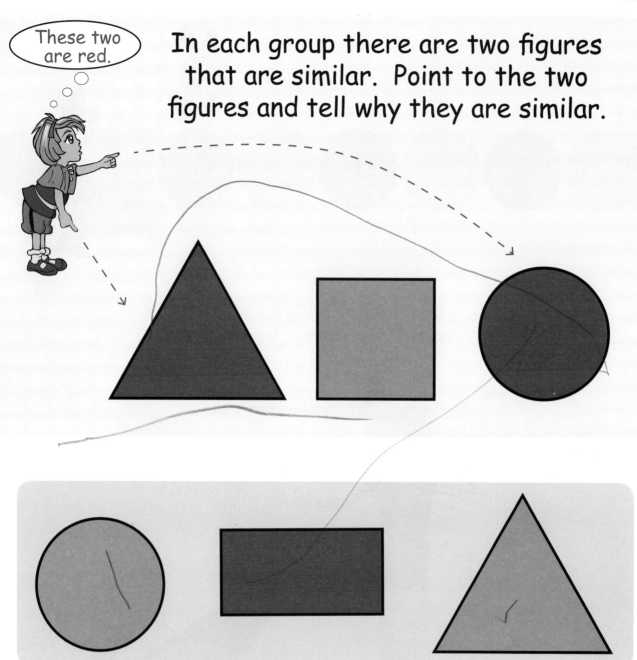

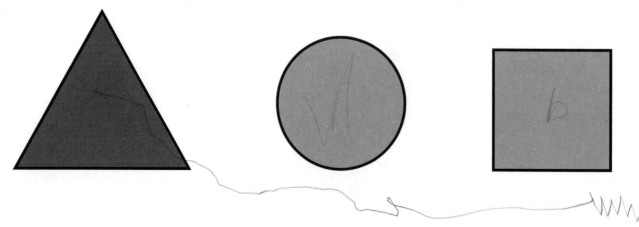

Someone said,
part of me is red,
but it isn't true,
I am all blue.

Of the four figures that you see,
tell me now, can you find me?

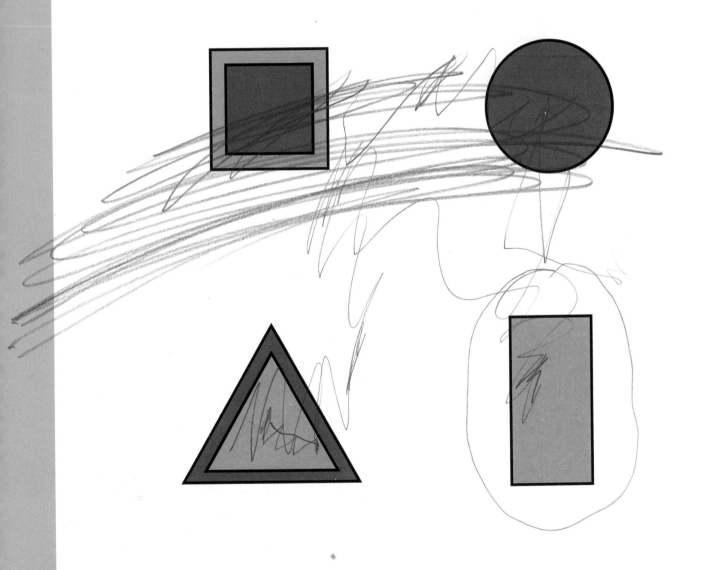

*For more activities like this, please see our *Can You Find Me?*™ series.

Identifying Colors

This figure is colored yellow.

Point to the yellow figure in each row.

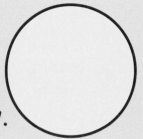

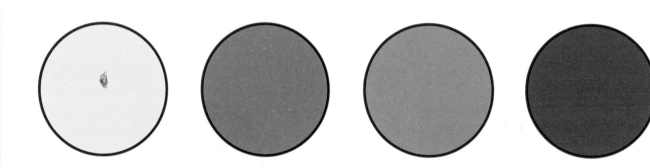

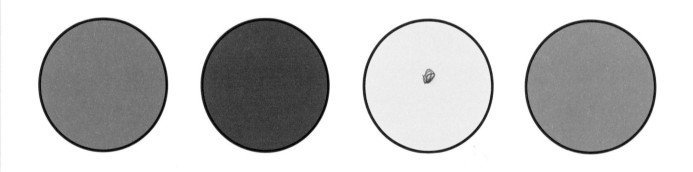

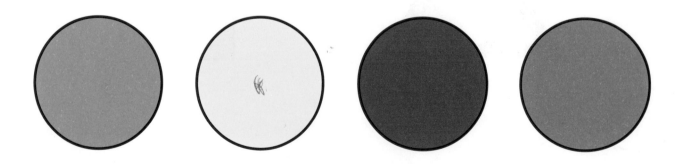

Identifying Colors

This figure is colored yellow.

Point to the yellow figure in each row.

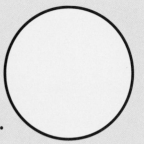

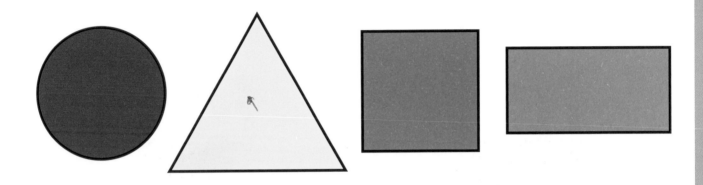

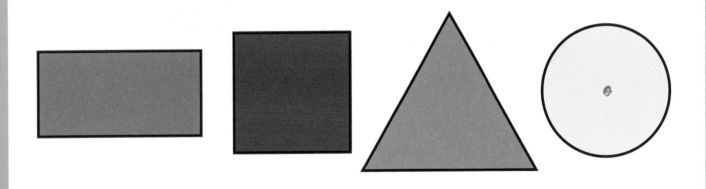

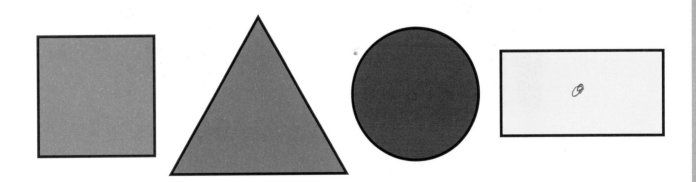

My hair is yellow,
My shirt is red.
I have no shoes,
I'm dressed for bed.

Of the four pictures that you see,
tell me now, can you find me?

*For more activities like this, please see our *Can You Find Me?*™ series.

Start here.

Draw a line connecting each yellow figure without touching any other color.

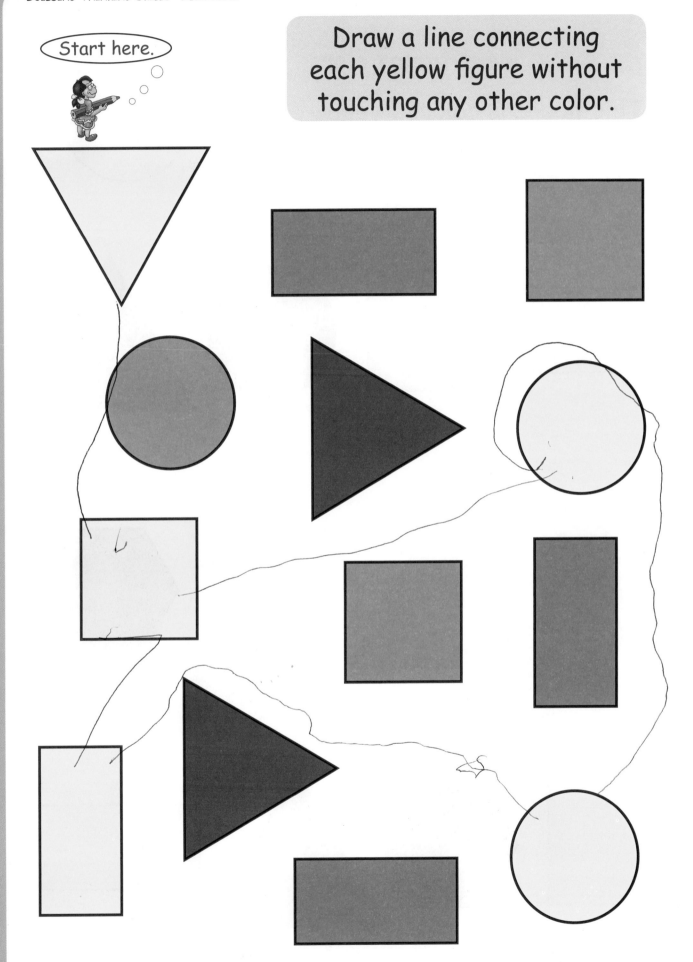

Identifying Colors

This figure is colored yellow.

Point to the yellow figures in each row.

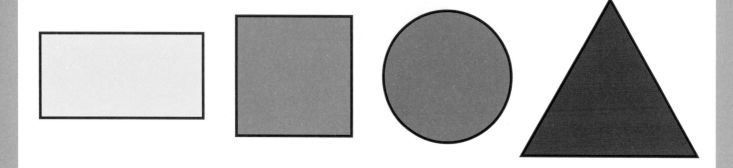

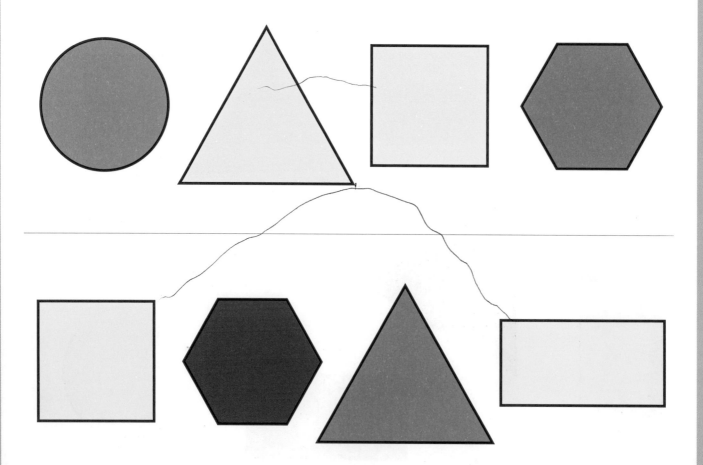

Point to the figure that I describe.

A red figure next to a yellow figure

A yellow figure next to a blue figure

A red figure next to a blue figure

Identifying Colors

Yellow

Blue

Red

Point to and say the color of each figure.

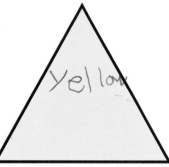

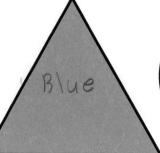

Find the path from the yellow figure to the blue figure.

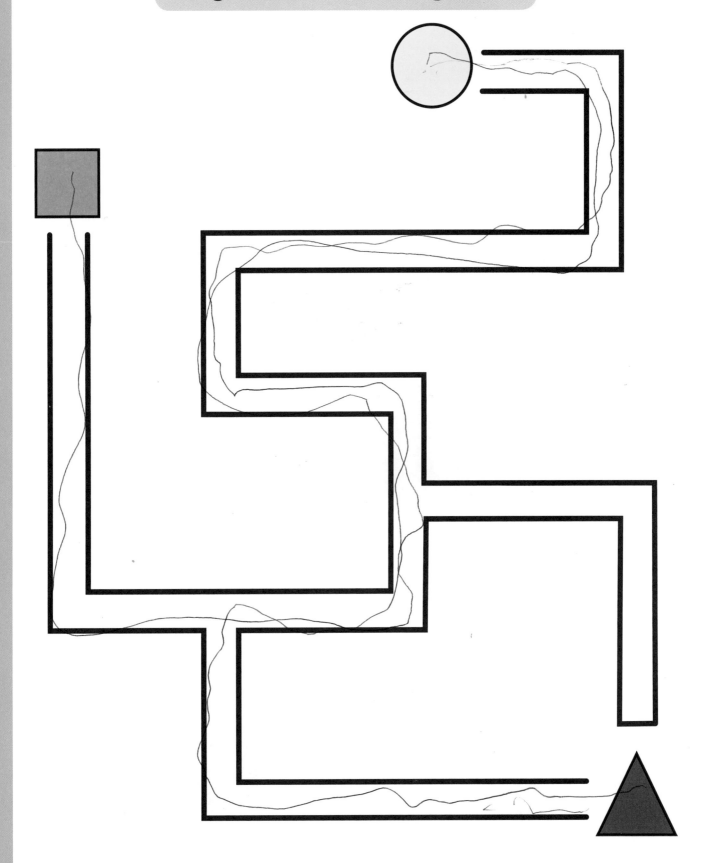

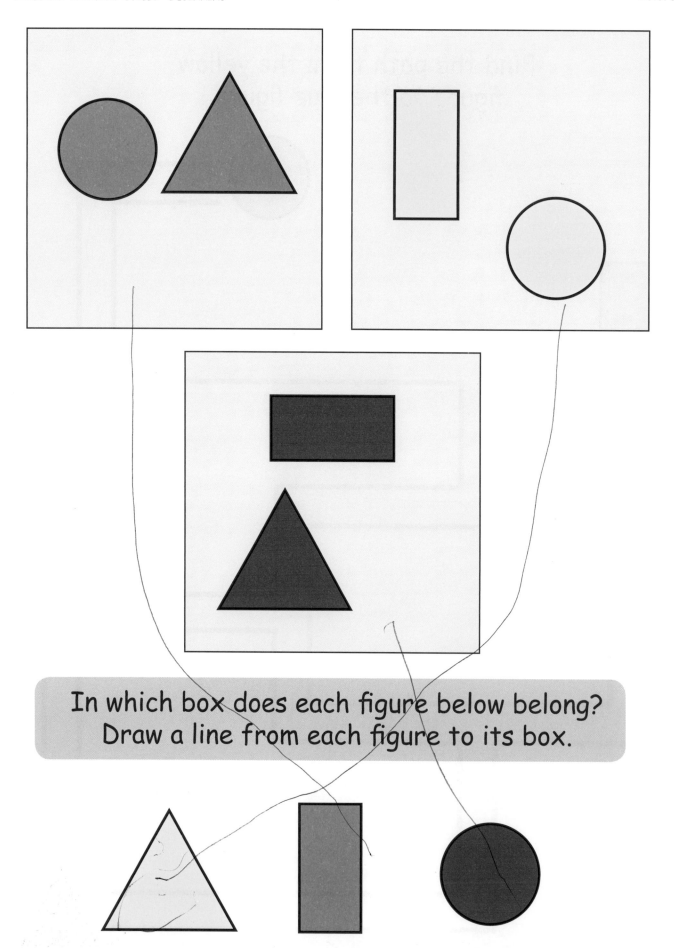

In which box does each figure below belong?
Draw a line from each figure to its box.

The cherries are red.
The plate is blue.
The applesauce is yellow,
and this plate is Sue's.

Of the four pictures that you see,
tell me now, can you find me?

*For more activities like this, please see our *Can You Find Me?*™ series.

Which shirt is red __and__ blue? _____

Which shirt is red __or__ blue? _____

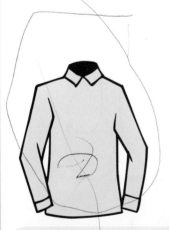   

Which shirt is yellow __or__ blue? _____

*Use your voice to emphasize the logical connecting "or" and "and" in each sentence.

Find the figure that doesn't belong. Then explain why it doesn't belong.

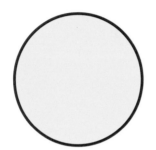 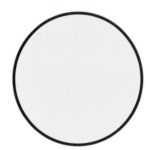 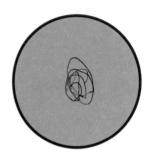

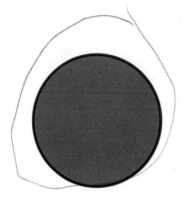  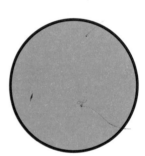

  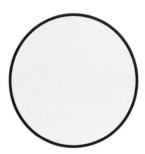

*Accept any answer that the student can logically defend.

I'm a larger fellow,
who always wears yellow.
I have just one shoe,
and it's colored blue.

Of the four pictures that you see,
tell me now, can you find me?

*For more activities like this, please see our *Can You Find Me?*™ series.

Identifying Colors

This figure is colored green.

Point to the green figure in each row.

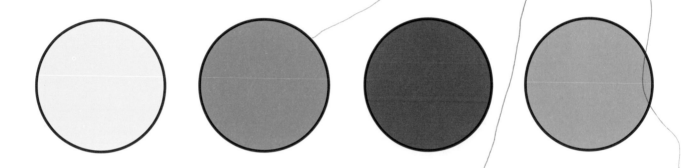

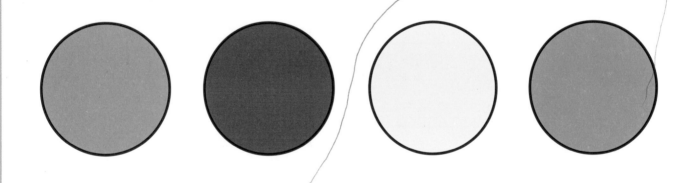

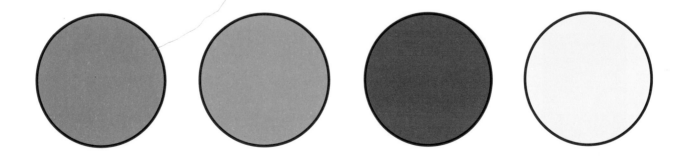

Identifying Colors

This figure is colored green.

Point to the green figure in each row.

My house is green,
the pond is blue,
a bird that's old,
a bird that's new.

Of the pictures that you see,
tell me now, can you find me?

*For more activities like this, please see our Can You Find Me?™ series.

Start here.

Draw a line connecting each green figure without touching any other color.

Identifying Colors

Yellow   Blue   Red   Green

Point to and say the color of each figure.

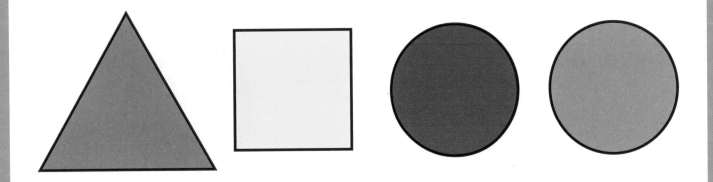

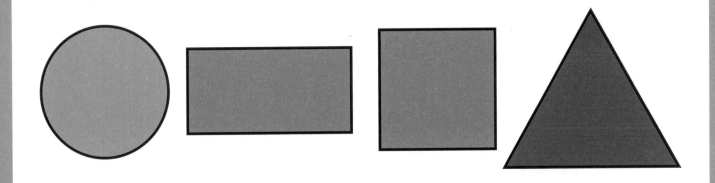

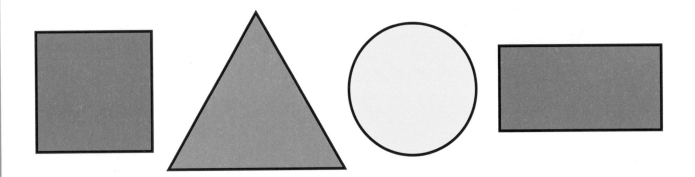

I am the color,
of the sun at the sea,
a very sour fruit,
or an autumn tree.

Of the four pictures that you see,
tell me now, can you find me?

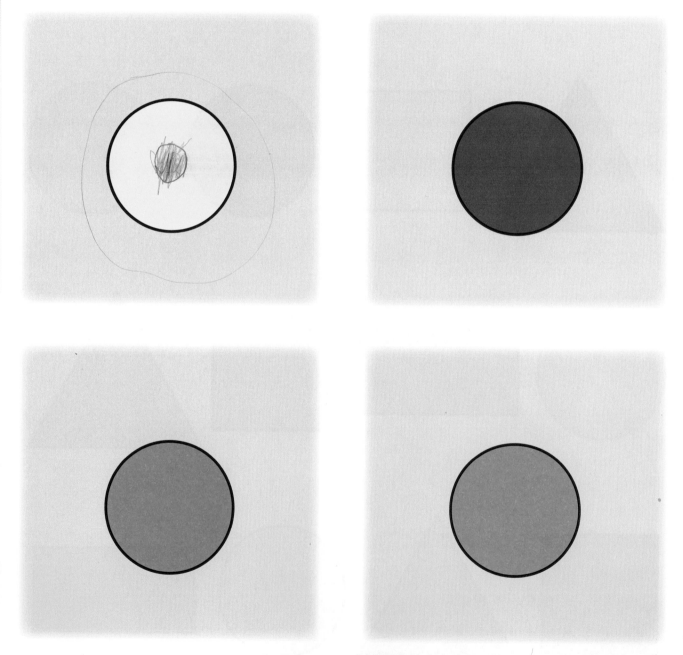

*For more activities like this, please see our *Can You Find Me?*™ series.

Building Thinking Skills® Beginning

Similarities and Differences

My head is green.
My nose is red.
I ate all my food,
so now I am fed.

Of the three pictures that you see,
tell me now, can you find me?

*For more activities like this, please see our *Can You Find Me?*™ series.

© 2008 The Critical Thinking Co.™ • www.CriticalThinking.com • 800-458-4849

35

✓

Identifying Colors

Yellow   Blue   Red   Green

Point to and say the color of each figure.

   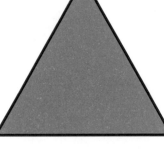

 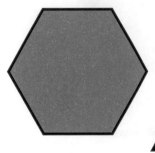 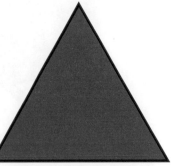

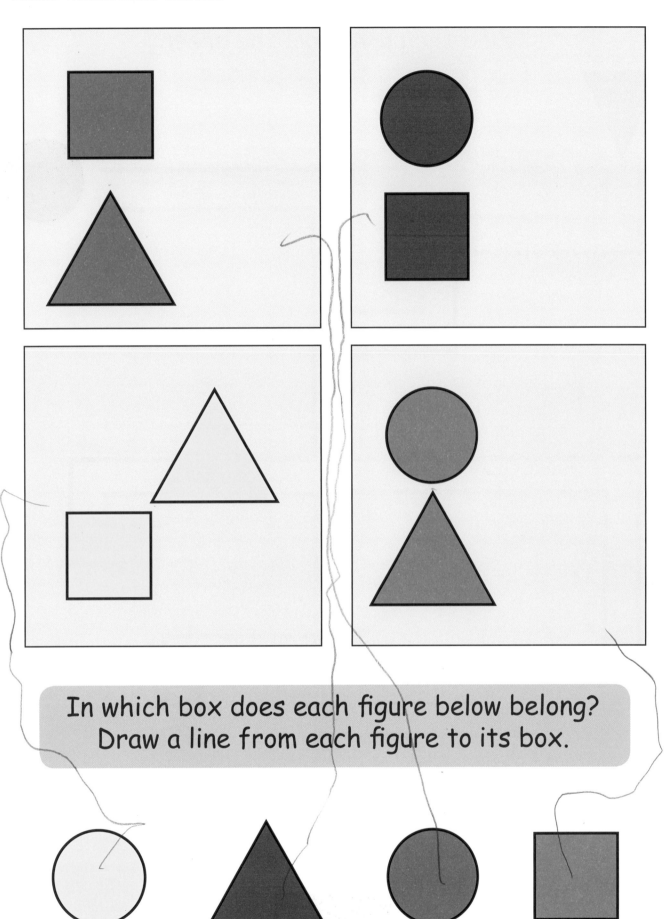

In which box does each figure below belong?
Draw a line from each figure to its box.

Find the path from the green figure to the red figure.

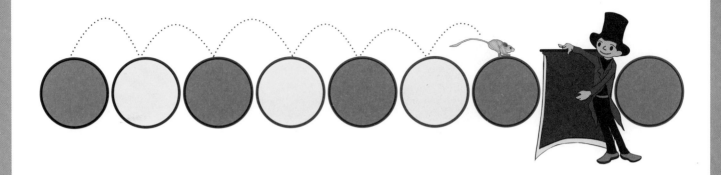

Say the color of each mouse jump.
What color is the boy hiding?

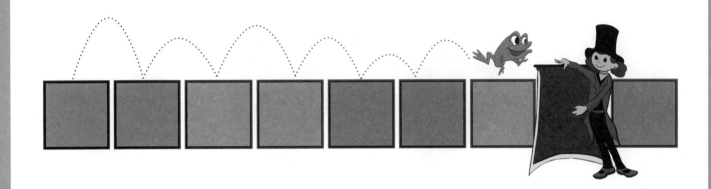

Say the color of each frog jump.
What color is the girl hiding?

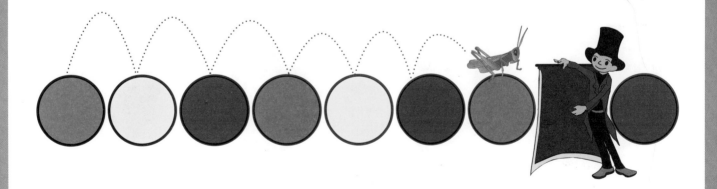

Say the color of each grasshopper jump.
What color is the boy hiding?

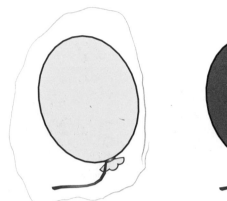   

Which balloon is green <u>or</u> yellow? _____

  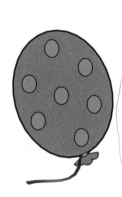 

Which balloon is green <u>and</u> yellow? _____

Which balloon is blue <u>or</u> green? _____

I'm quite a bit different,
from these other three.
See how they're alike,
then you will find me.

Of the four pictures that you see,
tell me now, can you find me?

*For more activities like this, please see our *Can You Find Me?*™ series.

Find the figure that doesn't belong.
Then explain why it doesn't belong.

*Accept any answer that the student can logically defend.

Describe one thing that is the same about both figures and one thing that is different.

*Accept any answer that the student can logically defend.

Identifying Lines

This is a straight line.

This is a curved line.

Point to each line below and say whether it is a straight or curved line.

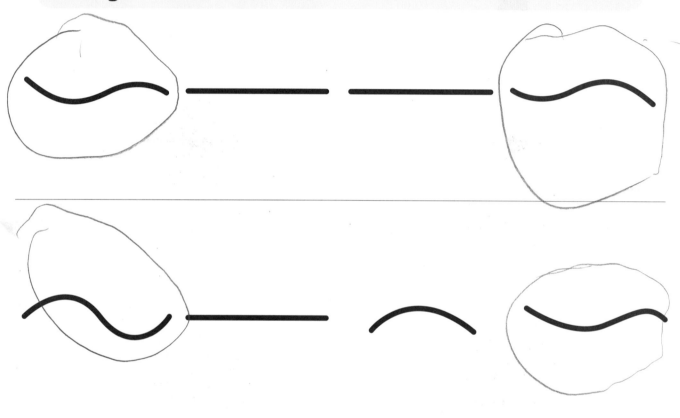

My head is curved.
My nose is straight.
I have a vegetable on my plate.

Of the four pictures that you see,
tell me now, can you find me?

*For more activities like this, please see our *Can You Find Me?*™ series.

Identifying Color and Line

Point to each line and say its color and whether it is straight or curved.

blue
curved line

Draw a line connecting each curved line without touching a straight line.

SGT

Identifying Color and Line

This is a straight line. ———

This is a curved line. ∿

This line is straight and curved. ⌐∿

Point to each line below and say its color and whether it is straight, curved, or straight and curved.

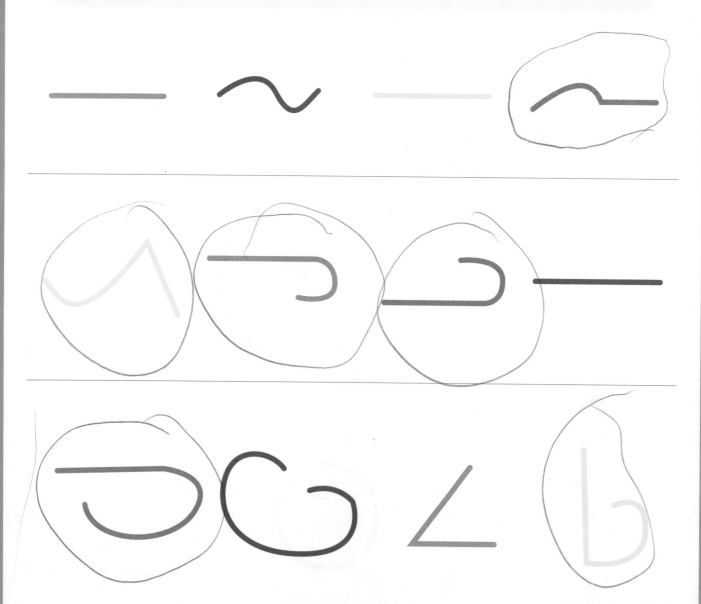

SGT

Point to the line I describe.

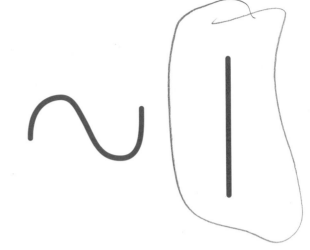

A red straight
line next to a
curved line

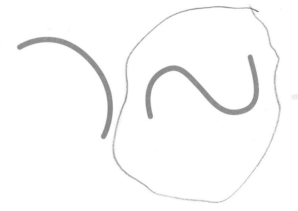

A blue curved
line next to a
straight line

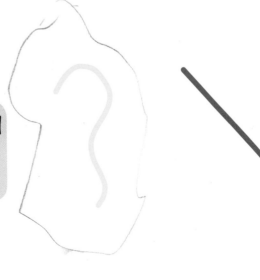

A yellow curved
line next to a
red line

SGT

I'm quite a bit different,
from these other three.
See how they're alike,
then you will find me.

Of the four pictures that you see,
tell me now, can you find me?

*For more activities like this, please see our *Can You Find Me?*™ series.

SGt

Find the figure that doesn't belong.
Then explain why it doesn't belong.

*Accept any answer that can be rationally defended by the student.

SGT

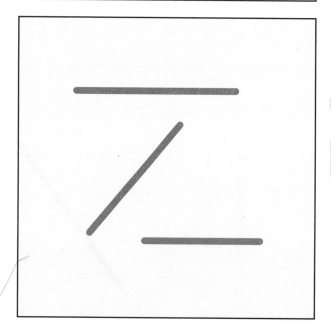

In which box does each figure below belong?
Draw a line from each figure to its box.

EFT SGT

Describe one thing that is the same about both figures and one thing that is different.

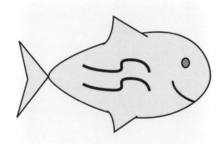
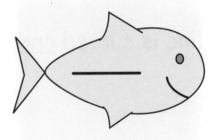

*Accept any answer that the student can logically defend.

Which line is blue or straight? _____

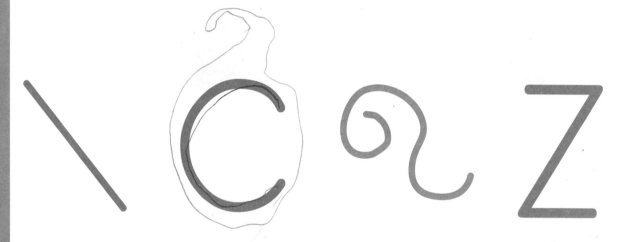

Which line is curved and green? _____

U S C 1

Which line is straight or yellow? _____

Identifying Lines

Straight Line	Curved Line	Straight and Curved Line
———	∼	⌒∼

Point to each line below and say whether it is straight, curved, or straight and curved.

Z P U T

L C E D

G I R W

Find the path from the straight blue line to the straight and curved line.

Point to the figure I describe.

A boy that just finished swimming next to a dog that just ate its food

A girl who ate a bowl of soup and sandwich next to a shorter boy

Look at each drawing below
and find it in the picture.

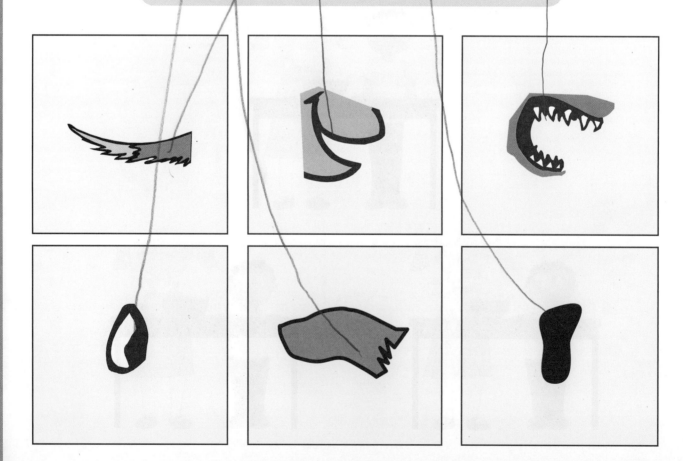

G

L   K
     T

Z   N   C
              S

In which box does each figure below belong?
Draw a line from each figure to its box.

V   U   M   O

Find the figure that doesn't belong.
Then explain why it doesn't belong.

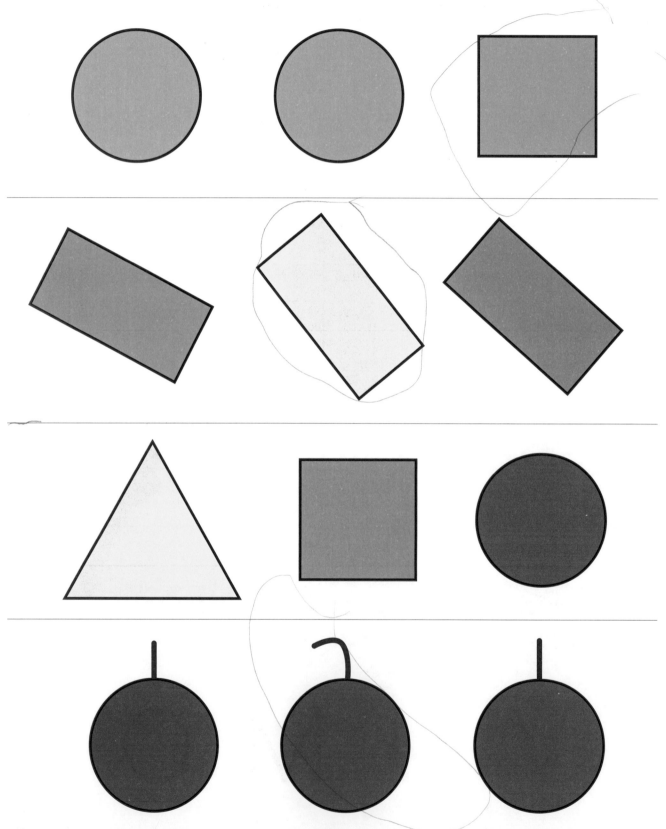

*Accept any answer that the student can logically defend.

VEFT

Identifying Lines

Straight Line	Curved Line	Straight and Curved Line

Point to each figure and say whether it is made of straight or curved lines.

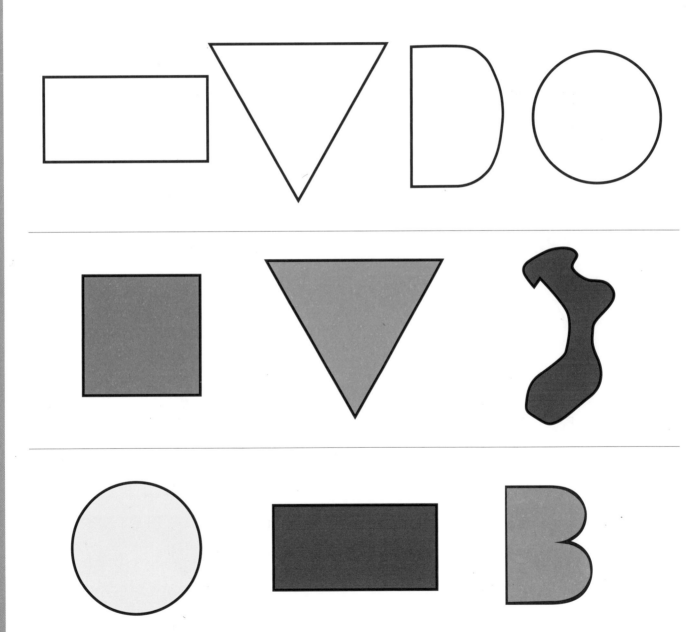

First I took a big sip,
and then another two.
My glass was almost empty,
when I was finally through.

Of the four glasses that you see,
which glass must belong to me?

*For more activities like this, please see our *Can You Find Me?*™ series.

Identifying Corners

These are corners.

A corner is the point where two straight lines meet. Point to each corner.

Point to the figure that matches my description.

Yes, it has a corner.

Red with three corners

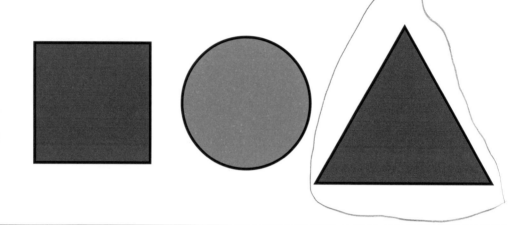

Green with no corners

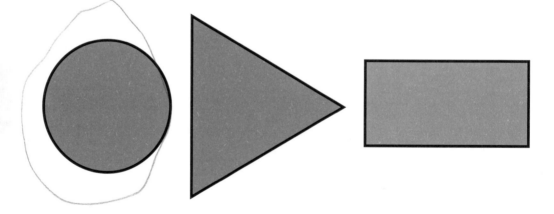

Yellow with three corners

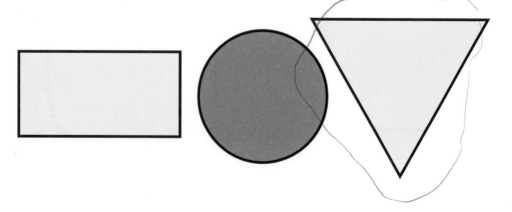

Point to the figure that matches the description.

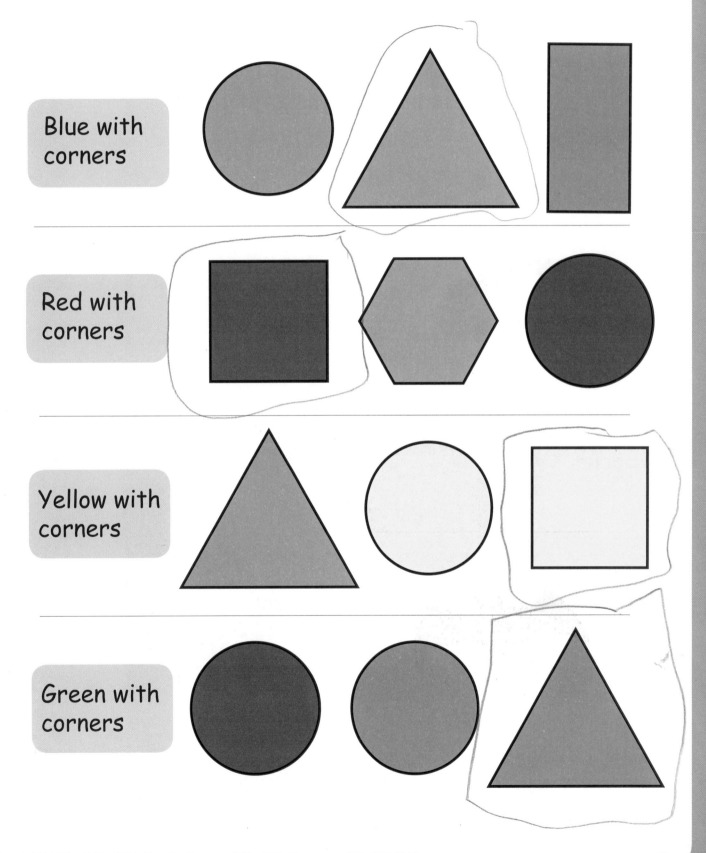

Blue with corners

Red with corners

Yellow with corners

Green with corners

A gray bat ate a blue bug.
A green snake ate the bat.
A red fox ate the snake,
and a fat, brown rat.

Of the four pictures that you see,
who is left in this story?

*For more activities like this, please see our *Can You Find Me?*™ series.

Point to the figure I describe.

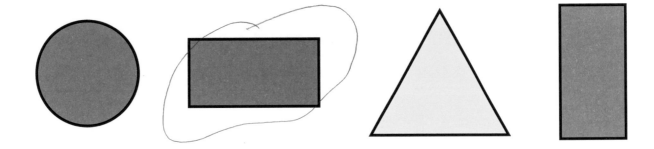

Green with corners _____

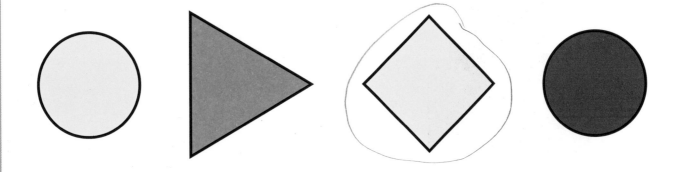

Yellow with straight lines _____

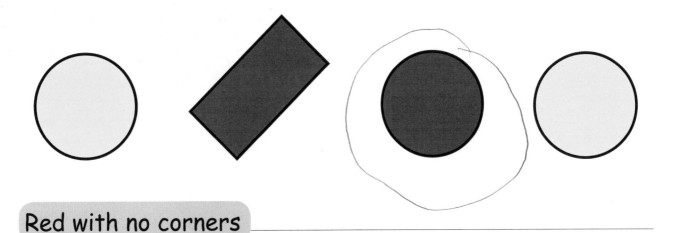

Red with no corners _____

Black and white,
above something blue.
A smell that's scary,
if it gets on you.

Of the four pictures that you see,
tell me now, can you find me?

*For more activities like this, please see our *Can You Find Me?*™ series.

Point to the figure I describe.

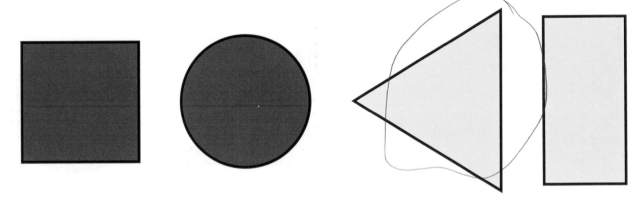

Yellow with corners next to red with curved lines

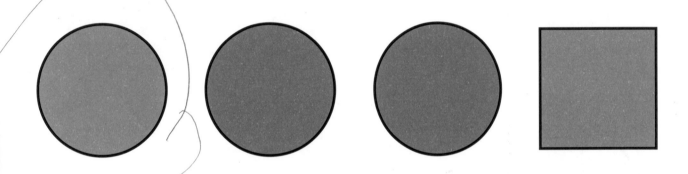

Blue with curved lines next to green with curved lines

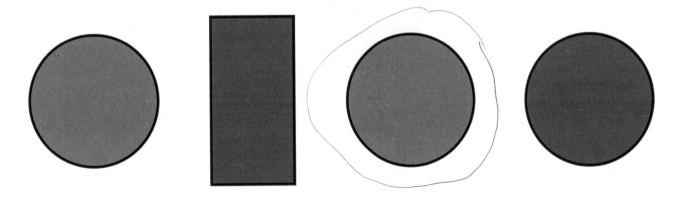

Green with curves next to red without corners

Start here.

Draw one line connecting each figure with a corner without touching any other figure.

Z   S   N

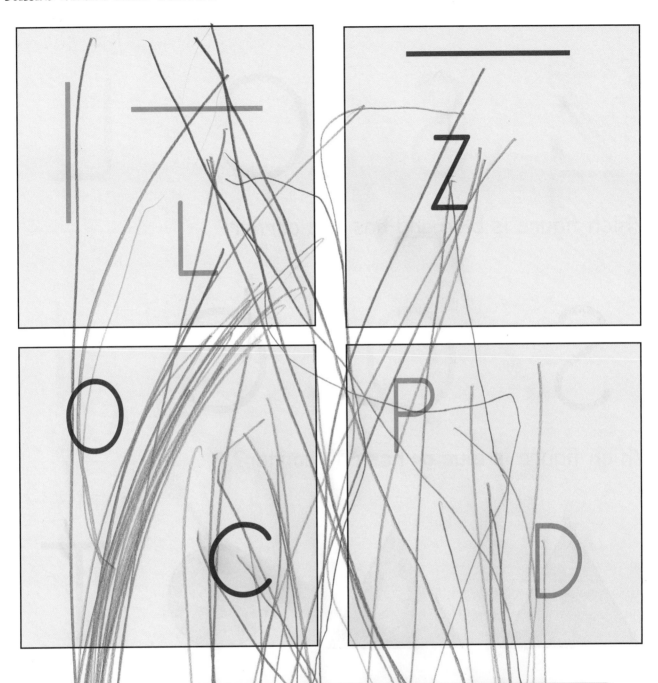

I

L

Z

O

P

C

D

In which box does each figure below belong?
Draw a line from each figure to its box.

Y   S   X   B

Z   S   C   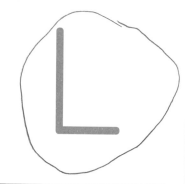

Which figure is blue **and** has one corner? _____

S   O   C   I

Which figure is blue **or** has one corner? _____

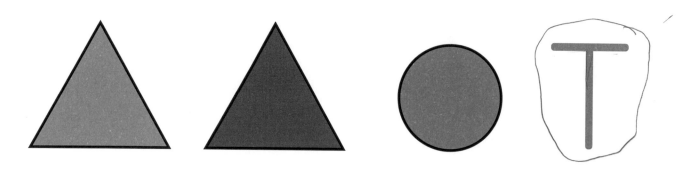

Which figure is green **and** has two corners? _____

S   Z   O   U

Which figure is green **or** has two corners? _____

Find the figure that doesn't belong.
Then explain why it doesn't belong.

⌐ | ⌐

C Q D

Z E O

| 3 6

*Accept any answer that the student can logically defend.

EFT

Describe one thing that is the same about both figures and one thing that is different.

*Accept any answer that the student can logically defend.

Find the path from the green figure with corners to the red figure without corners.

EFT

This shape is a circle. Point to each circle and say its color and shape.

blue circle

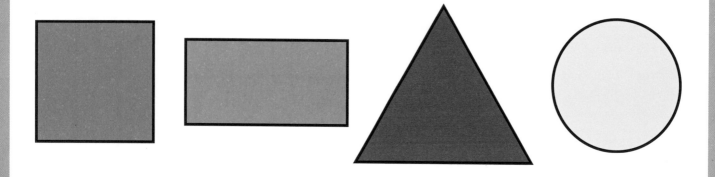

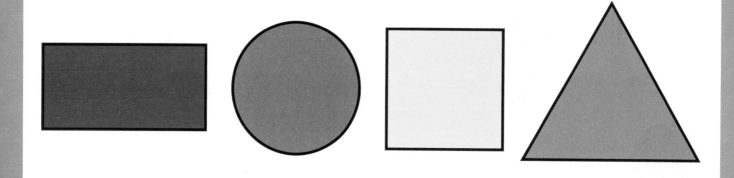

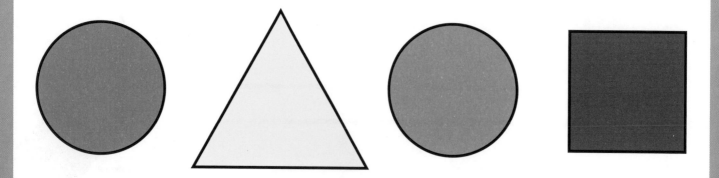

EFT

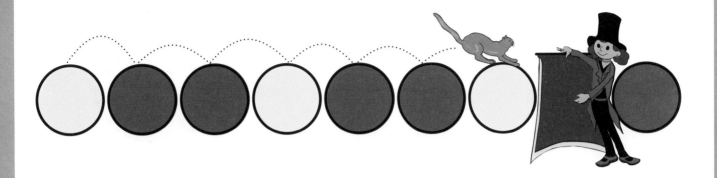

Say the color of each cat jump.
What color and shape is the girl hiding?

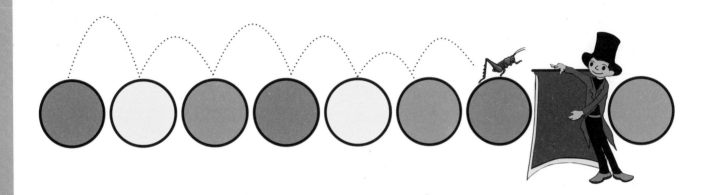

Say the color of each cricket jump.
What color and shape is the boy hiding?

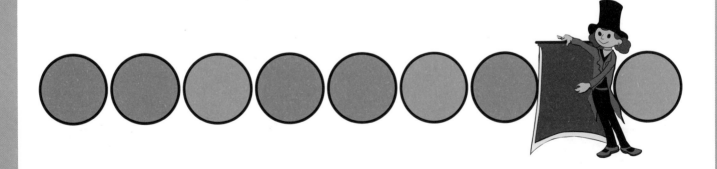

What color and shape is the girl hiding?

EFT

Point to each circle and say its color and shape.

red circle

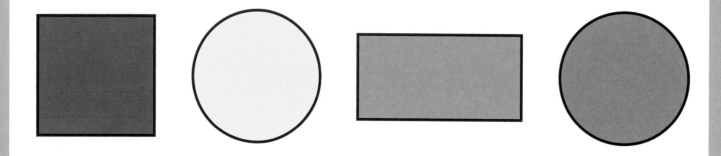

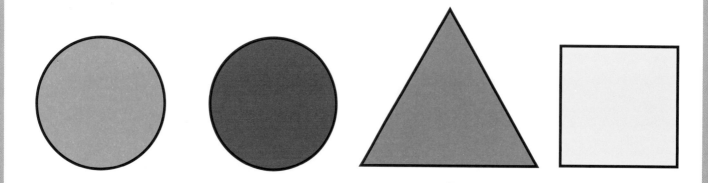

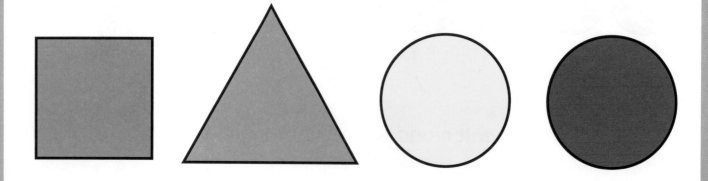

EFT

79

Answer the following questions.

1. Does a circle have a straight line?

2. Does a circle have a curved line?

3. Does a circle have a corner?

Point to each circle in the picture below and say its color and shape.

Find the pair of figures I describe.

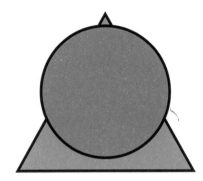 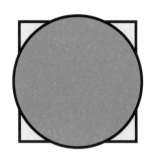 

A blue circle in front of a green figure

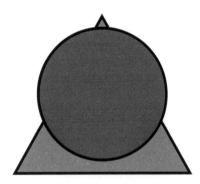  

A red circle in front of a figure with corners

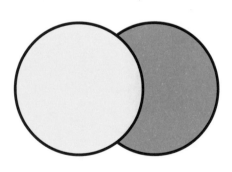 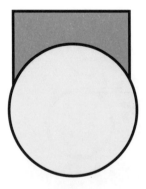 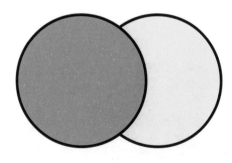

A yellow circle in front of a blue figure with curved lines

V

Find the figure that doesn't belong. Then explain why it doesn't belong.

 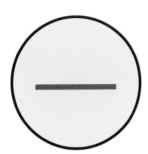 

Z M G

T X R

*Accept any answer that the student can logically defend.

Start here.

Draw a line connecting each circle without touching any other shape.

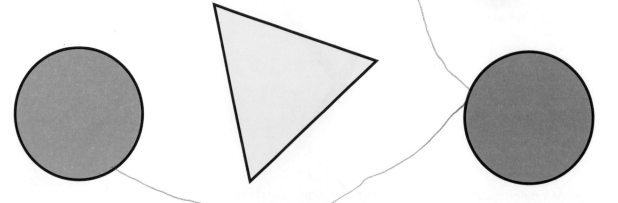

Find the path from the blue circle to the red figure with corners.

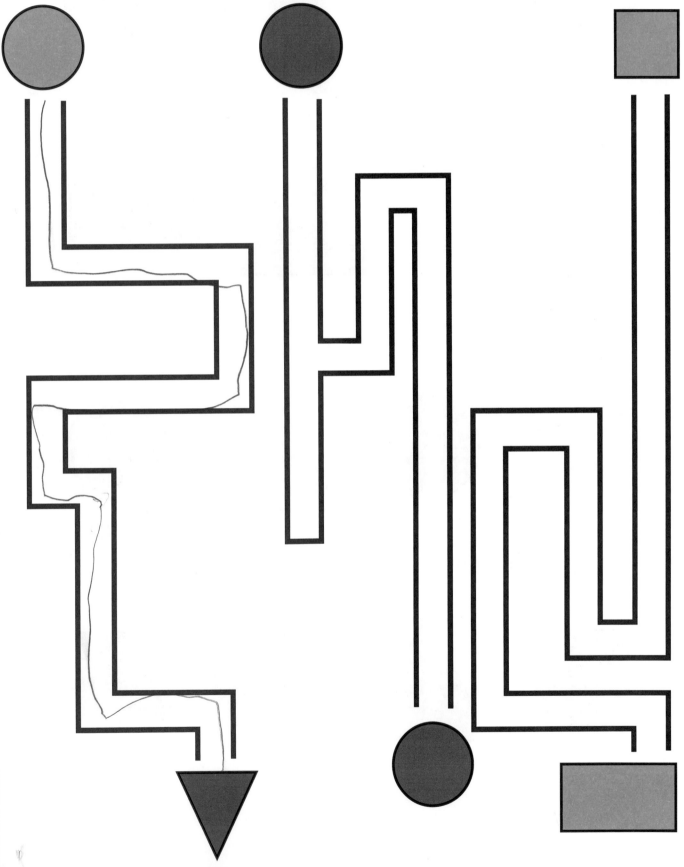

EFT

 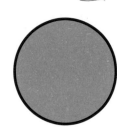  

Which figure is a circle <u>and</u> blue? _____

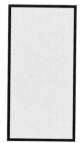  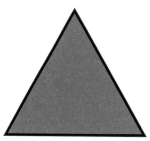 

Which figure is a circle <u>or</u> red? _____

  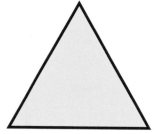 

Which figure is a circle <u>and</u> yellow? _____

 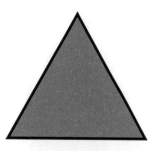  

Which figure is blue <u>or</u> a circle? _____

In which box does each figure below belong?
Draw a line from each figure to its box.

FFT

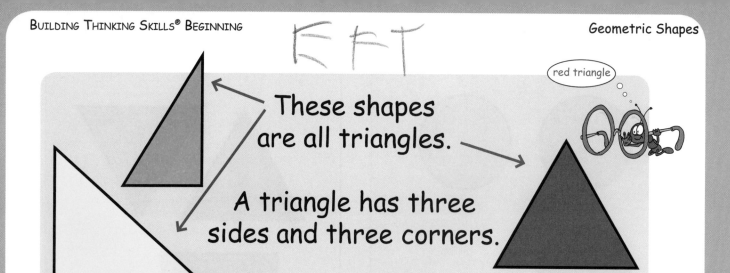

These shapes are all triangles.

A triangle has three sides and three corners.

red triangle

Point to and say the color and shape of each figure below.

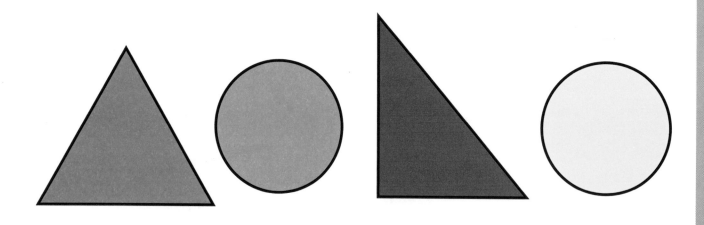

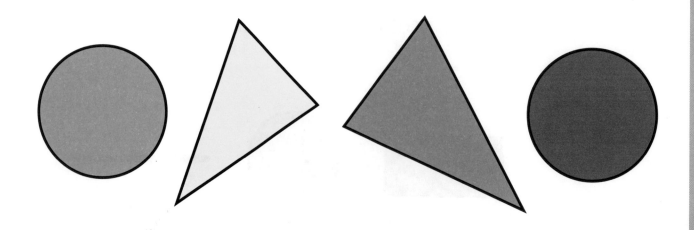

EFT

Point to each figure and say its color and shape.

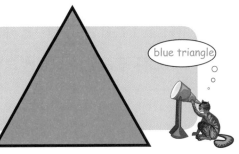

blue triangle

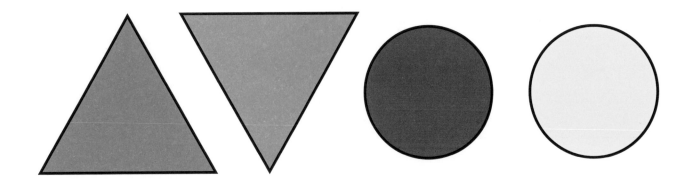

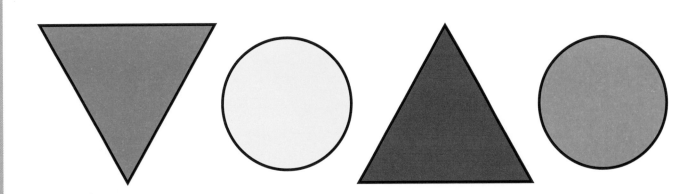

Find the figure that doesn't belong. Then explain why it doesn't belong.

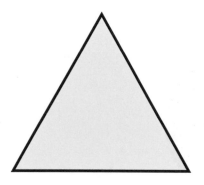 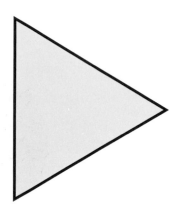 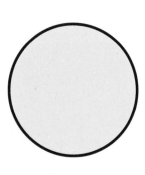

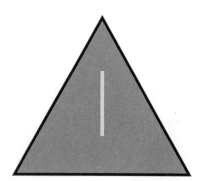  

*Accept any answer that the student can logically defend.

Describe one thing that is the same about both figures and one thing that is different.

 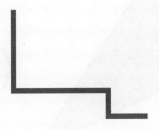

*Accept any answer that the student can logically defend.

Point to each figure and
say its color and shape.

red triangle

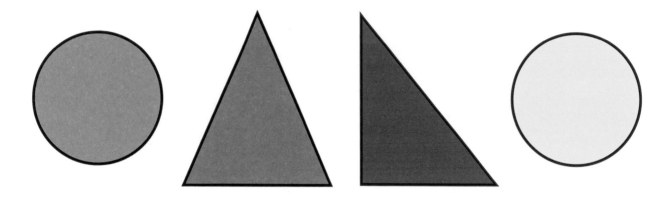

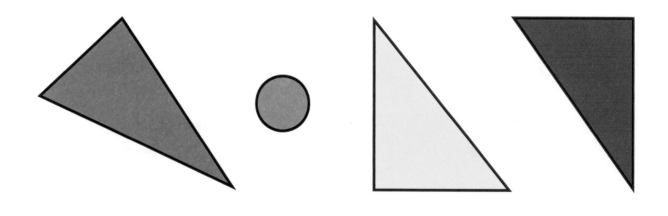

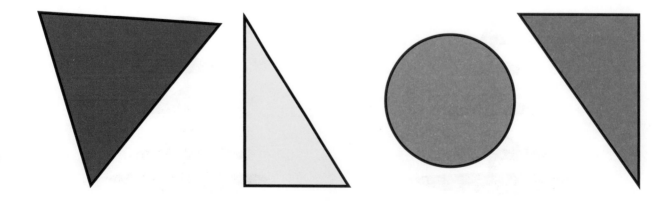

Point to the figure that I describe.

A red triangle next to a green circle

A yellow circle next to a blue circle

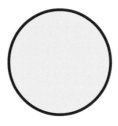 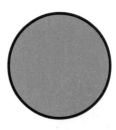 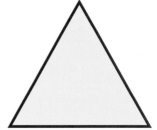

A green triangle next to a blue circle

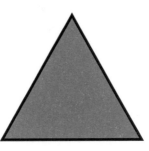 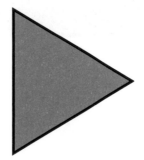 

A red circle in between two circles

EFT

I have three corners,
but I am not blue.
I'm above red,
and those are your clues.

Of the four figures that you see,
tell me now, can you find me?

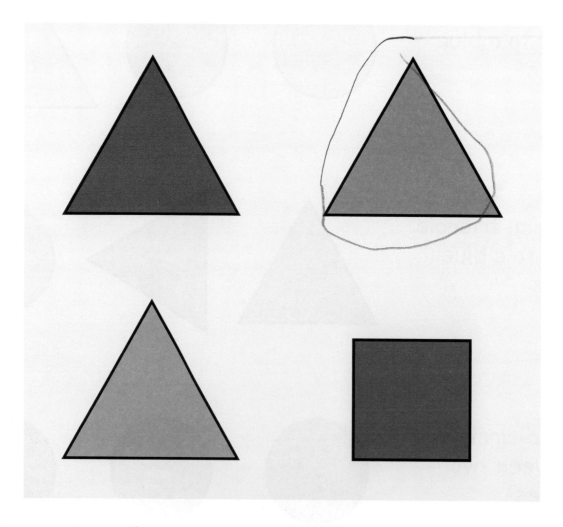

*For more activities like this, please see our *Can You Find Me?*™ series.

Start here.

Draw a line connecting each triangle without touching any other shape.

EFT

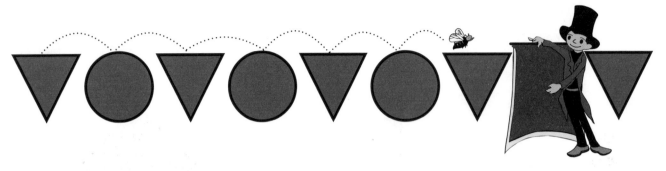

Say the shape of each flea jump.
What shape is the boy hiding?

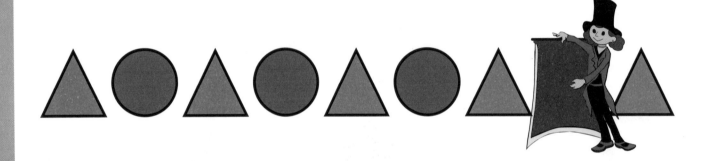

What color and shape is the girl hiding?

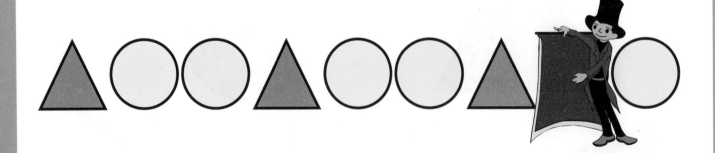

What color and shape is the boy hiding?

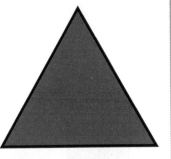

Answer the following questions yes or no.

1. Does a triangle have curves?
2. Does a triangle have a straight line?
3. Does a triangle have more than one straight line?
4. Does a triangle have a straight and curved line?
5. Does a triangle have a corner?
6. Does a triangle have more than one corner?

Point to each triangle in the picture.

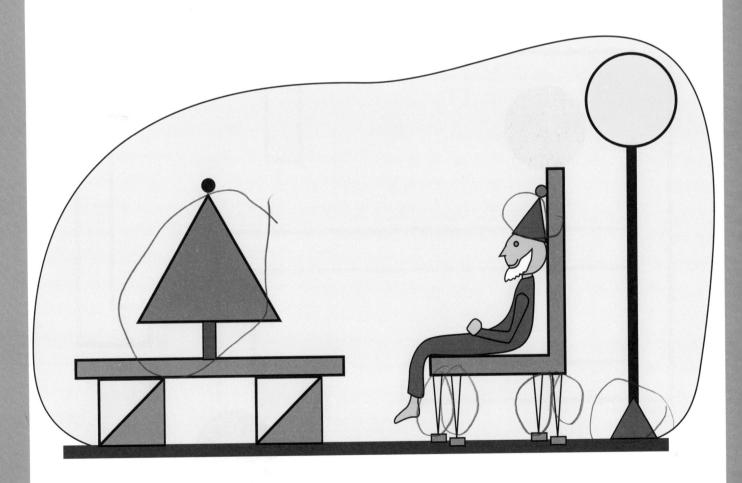

Find the path from the red triangle to the green circle.

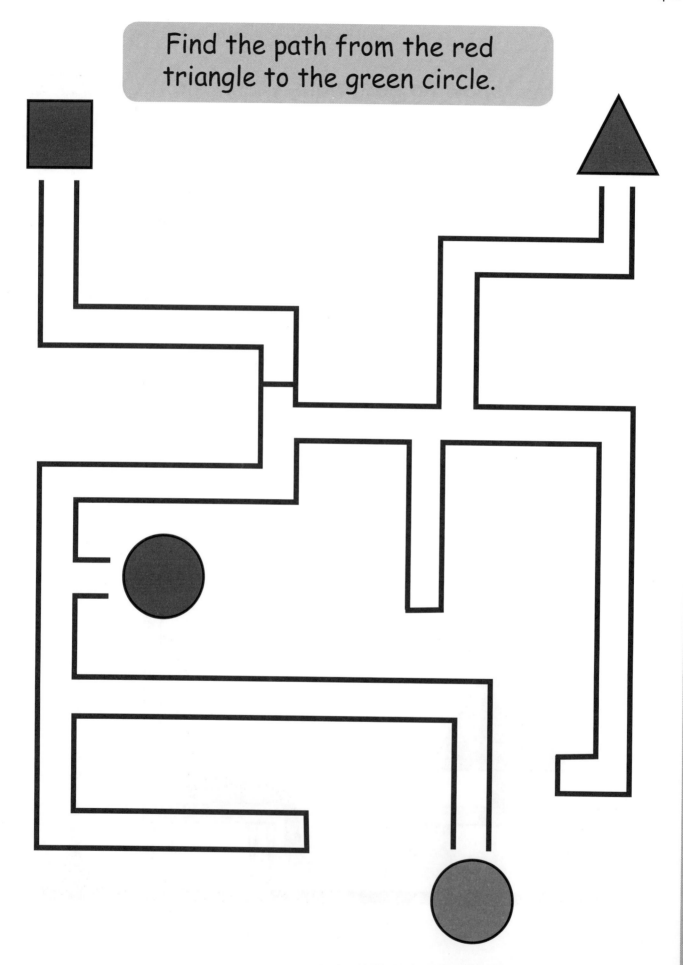

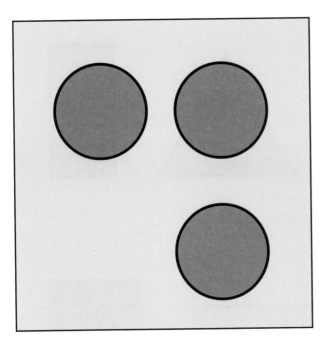

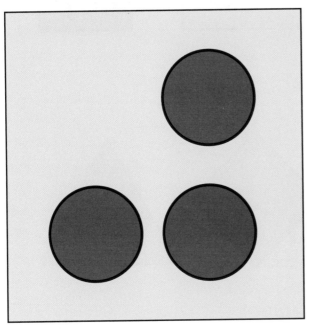

In which box does each figure below belong? Draw a line from each figure to its box.

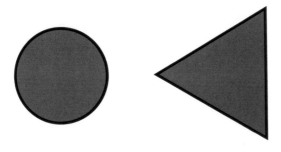

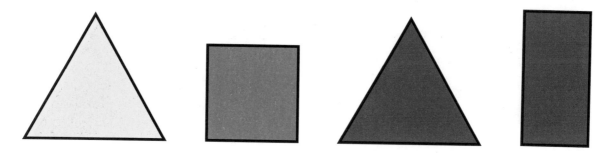

Which figure is red <u>and</u> a triangle? _____

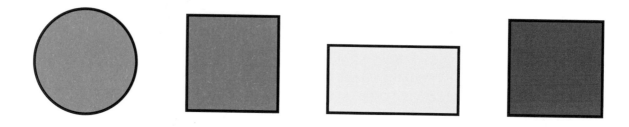

Which figure is red <u>or</u> a triangle? _____

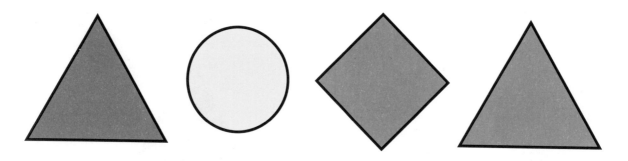

Which figure is blue <u>and</u> a triangle? _____

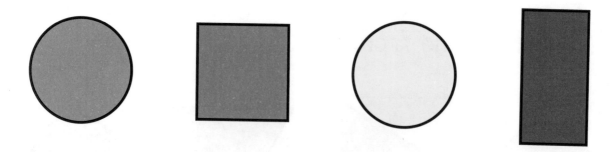

Which figure is blue <u>or</u> a triangle? _____

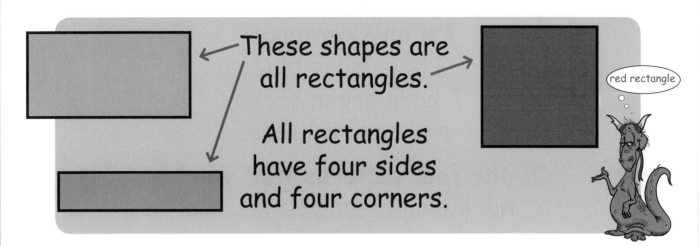

These shapes are all rectangles.

red rectangle

All rectangles have four sides and four corners.

Point to and say the color and shape of each figure below.

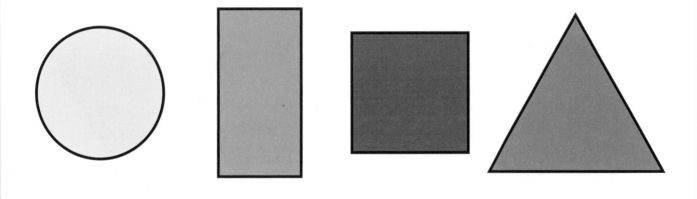

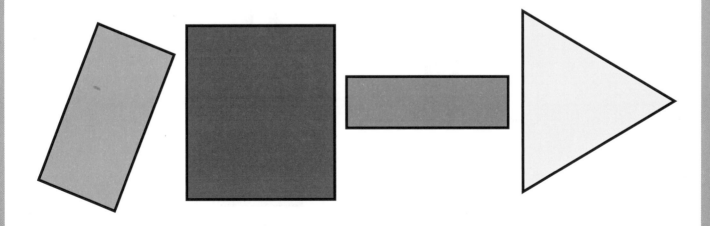

I'm on a rectangle.
Its color is blue.
I have green socks,
and one red shoe.

Of the four pictures that you see,
tell me now, can you find me?

*For more activities like this, please see our *Can You Find Me?*™ series.

Point to and say the color and
shape of each figure below.

green rectangle

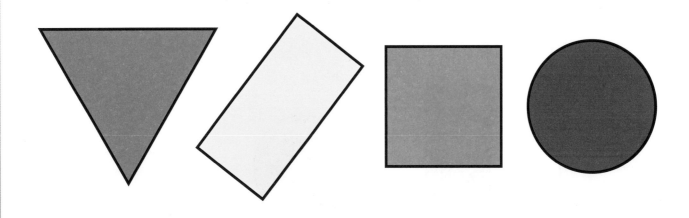

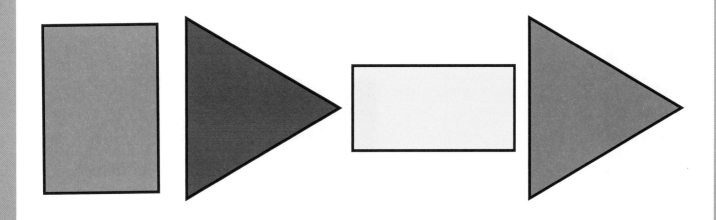

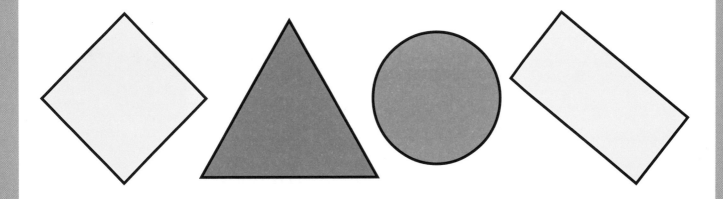

Point to the figure I describe.

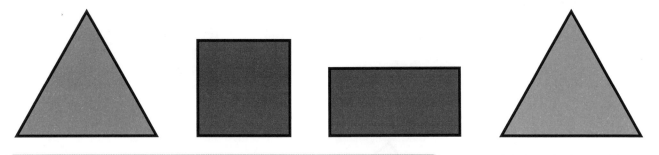

A red rectangle next to a blue triangle _____

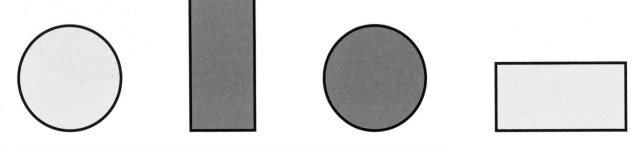

A green circle next to a yellow rectangle _____

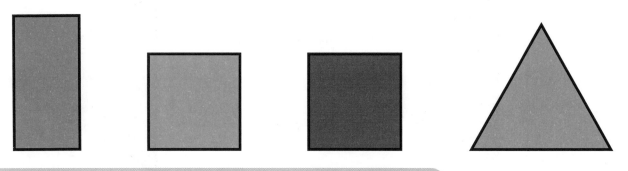

A blue rectangle next to a red rectangle _____

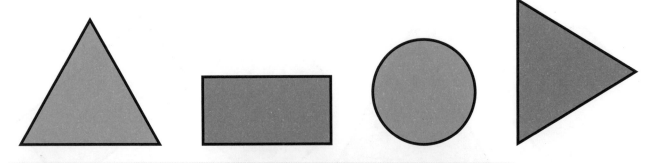

A green rectangle next to a figure with curves _____

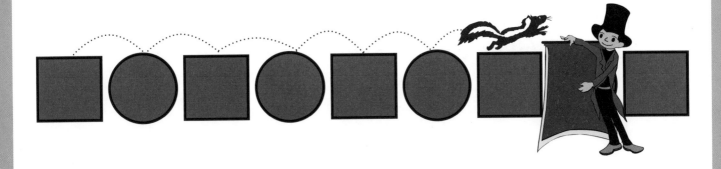

Say the shape of each skunk jump.
What shape is the boy hiding?

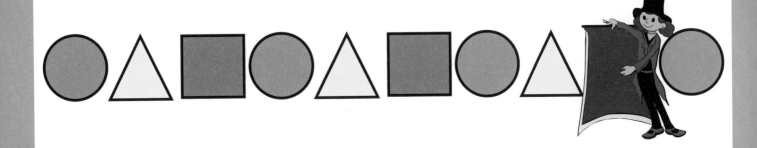

What color and shape is the girl hiding?

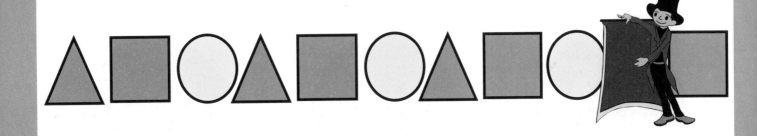

What color and shape is the boy hiding?

Find the figure that doesn't belong. Then explain why it doesn't belong.

 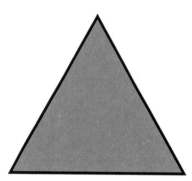 

W   T   P

*Accept any answer that the student can logically defend.

red rectangle

Point to and say the color and shape of each figure below.

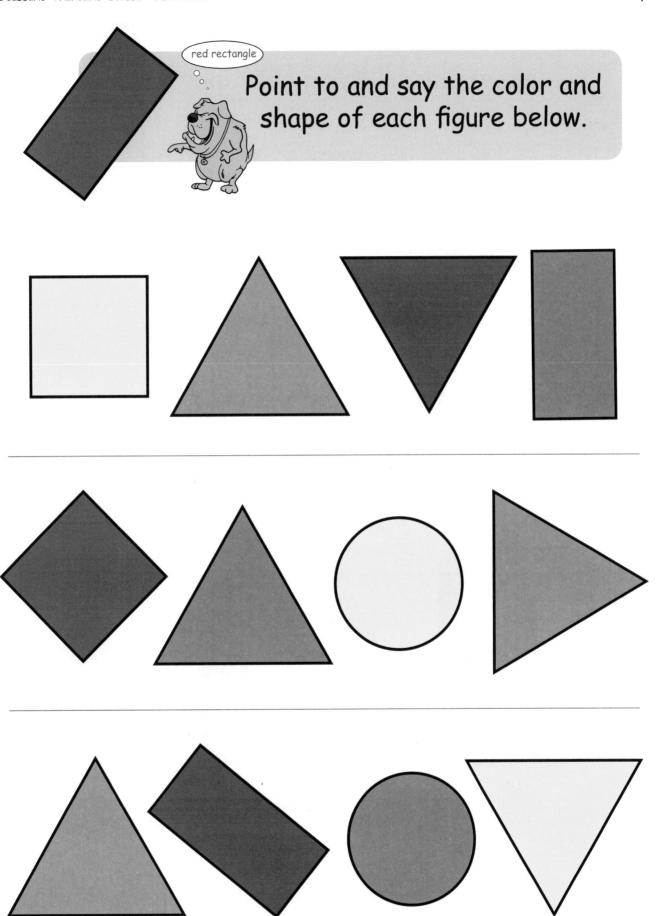

EFT

Answer the following questions.

1. Does a rectangle have a straight line?
2. Does a rectangle have more than one straight line?
3. Does a rectangle have a curved line?
4. Does a rectangle have a corner?
5. Does a rectangle have more than one corner?

Point to each rectangle in the picture.

FFT

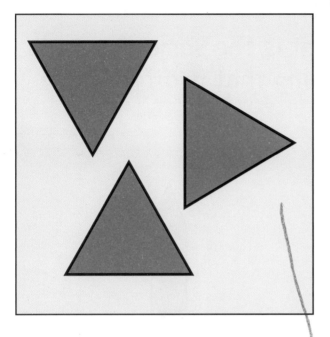

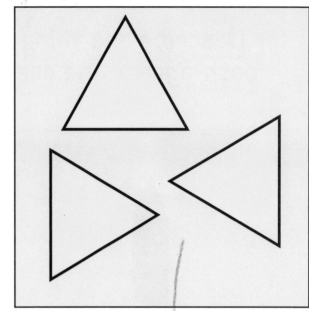

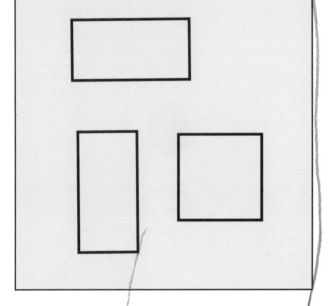

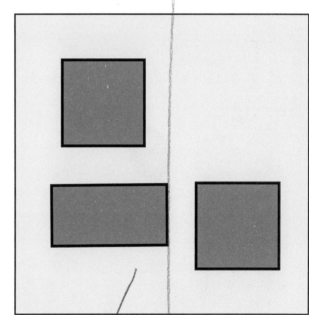

In which box does each figure below belong?
Draw a line from each figure to its box.

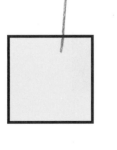

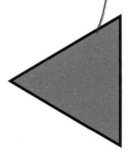

EFT

Describe one thing that is the same about both figures and one thing that is different.

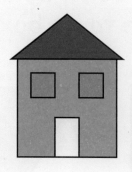 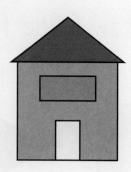

*Accept any answer that the student can logically defend.

EFt

Start here.

Draw a line connecting each rectangle without touching any other shape.

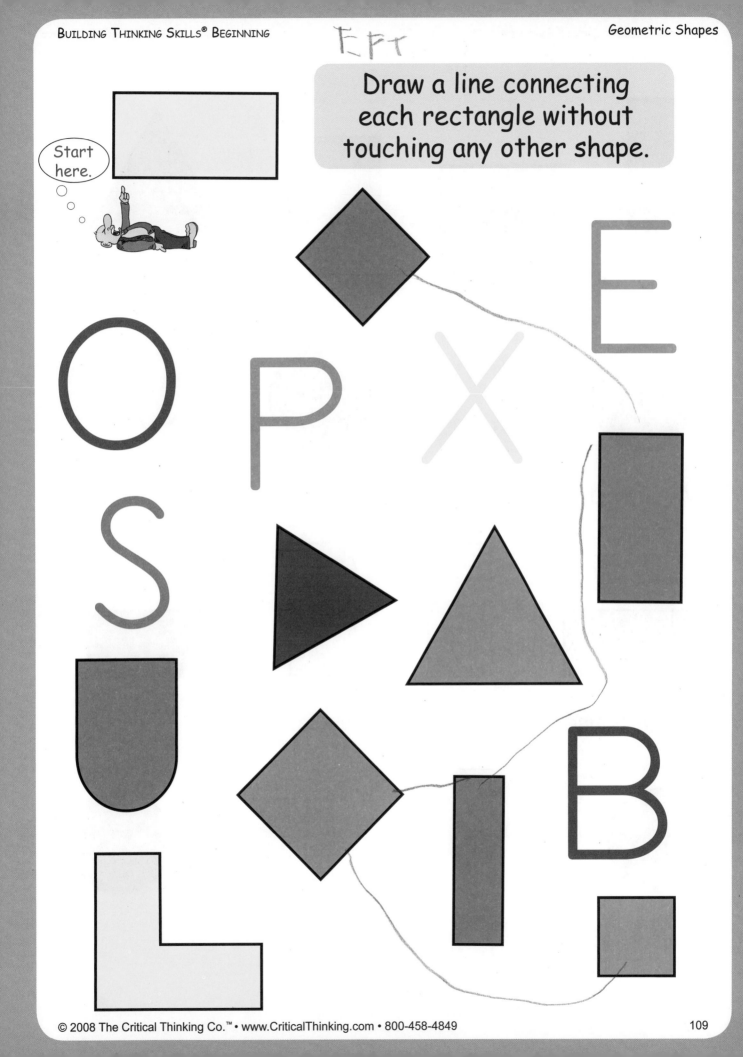

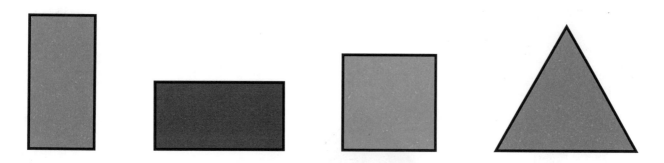

Which figure is a rectangle <u>and</u> green? _____

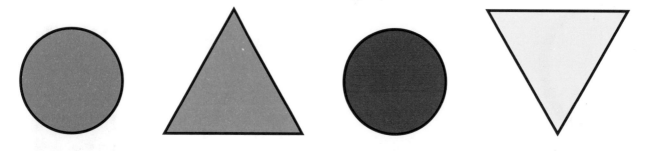

Which figure is a rectangle <u>or</u> green? _____

Which figure is yellow <u>and</u> a rectangle? _____

Which figure is yellow <u>or</u> a rectangle? _____

Find the path from the blue rectangle to the blue triangle.

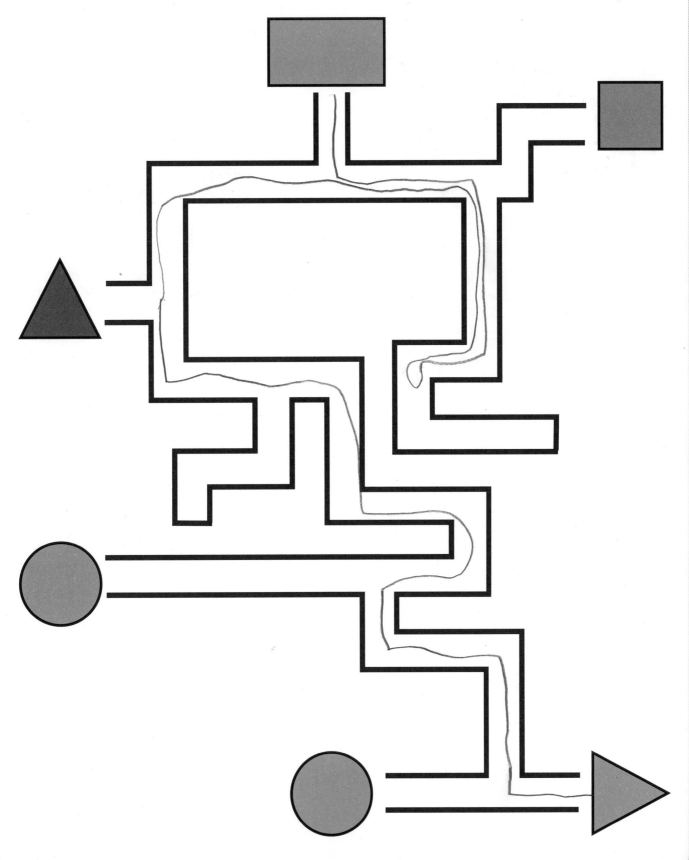

Look at each face above, then find its
unfinished picture below. Use a pencil
to draw in all the missing parts.

Color the pictures when you
are finished drawing.

*For more activities like this, please see our *Thinker Doodles*™ series.

EFT

These shapes are special rectangles called squares. Each side of a square is the same.

Point to and say the color and shape of each figure below.

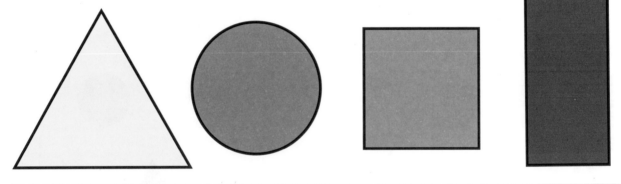

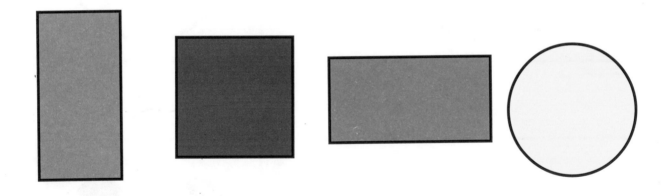

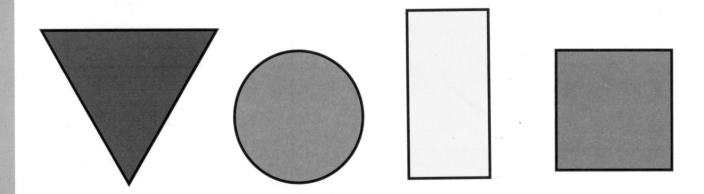

My nose is a triangle.
My head is a square.
I look through blue eyes,
to see you there.

Of the four pictures that you see,
tell me now, can you find me?

*For more activities like this, please see our *Can You Find Me?*™ series.

Start here.

Draw a line connecting each square without touching any other shape.

Which shape in each group is not a square?

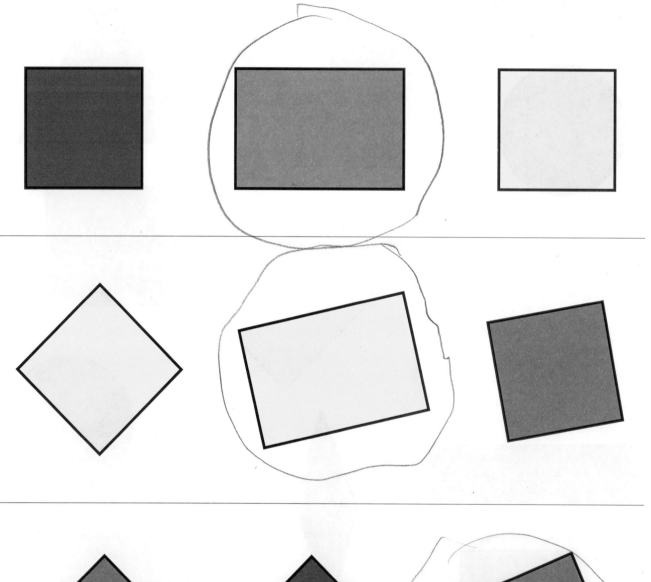

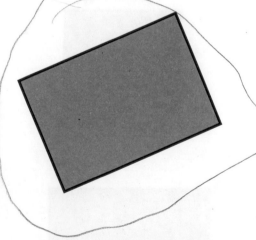

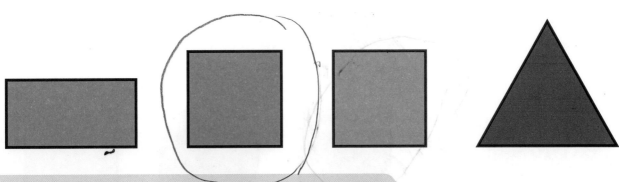

Which figure is a square <u>and</u> green? _____

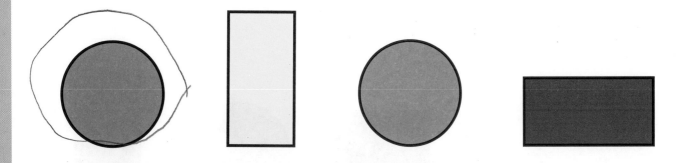

Which figure is a square <u>or</u> green? _____

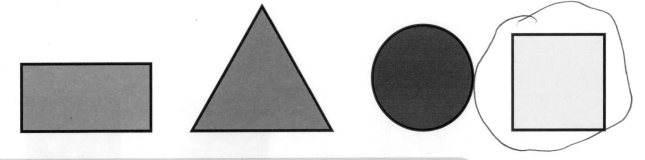

Which figure is a rectangle <u>and</u> a square? _____

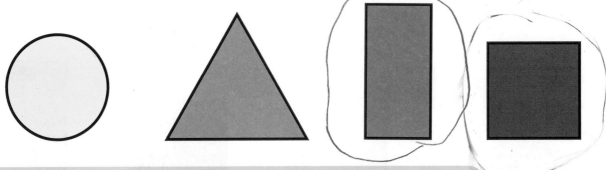

Which figure is a rectangle <u>or</u> a blue square? _____

Point to the figure that I describe.

A yellow square next to a green circle

A red square next to a blue circle

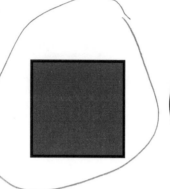  

A green square next to a blue rectangle

A blue rectangle next to a green rectangle

  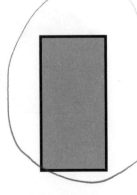

Point to the figure that I describe.

A red rectangle next to a green square

A blue square next to a yellow triangle

A yellow square next to a yellow circle

A blue rectangle next to a green square

FFT

My eyes are rectangles.
My blue nose is square.
I have sharp teeth,
so you'd better beware.

Of the four things that you see,
tell me now, can you find me?

*For more activities this is, please see our *Can You Find Me?*™ series.

Find the figure that doesn't belong.
Then explain why it is different.

Find the path from the blue square to the yellow rectangle.

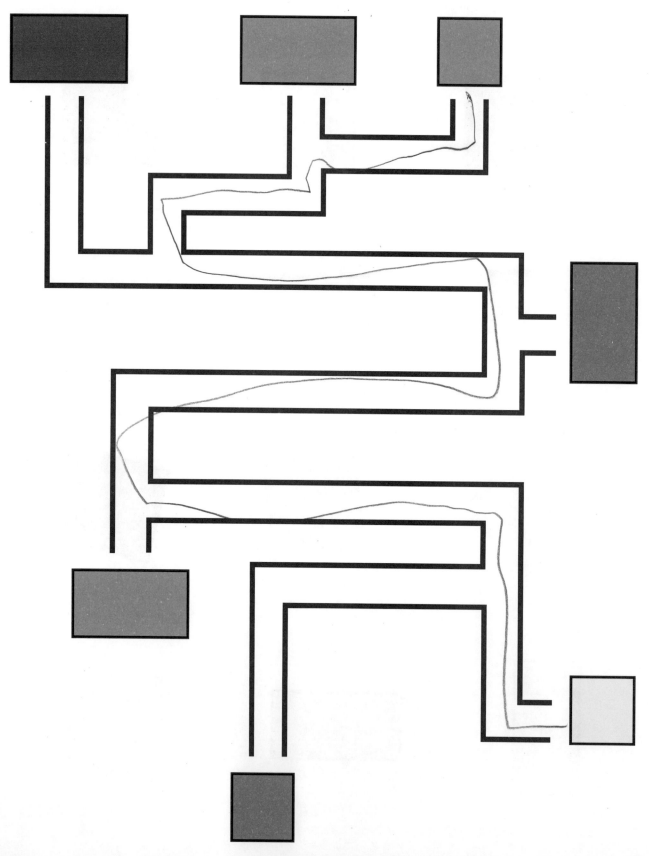

EFT

Describe one thing that is the same about both figures and one thing that is different.

 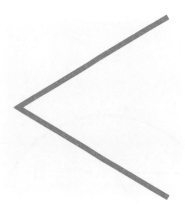

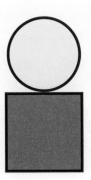 

*Accept any answer that the student can logically defend.

Look at each face above, then find
its unfinished picture below. Use a
pencil to draw the missing parts.

Color the pictures when you
are finished drawing.

*For more activities like this, please see our *Thinker Doodles*™ series.

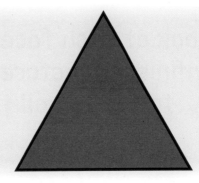

Which pictures below are made with the two figures above?

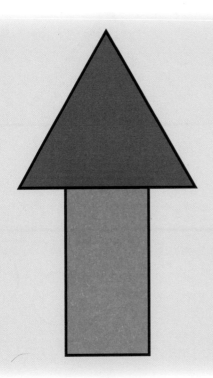

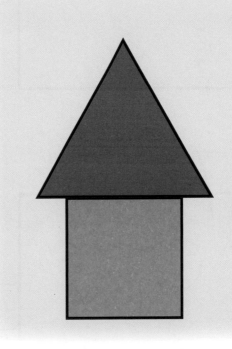

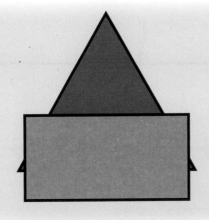

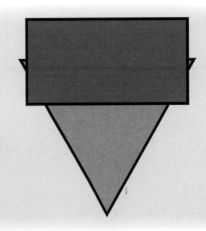

Look at each face above, then find its unfinished picture below. Use a pencil to draw in all the missing parts.

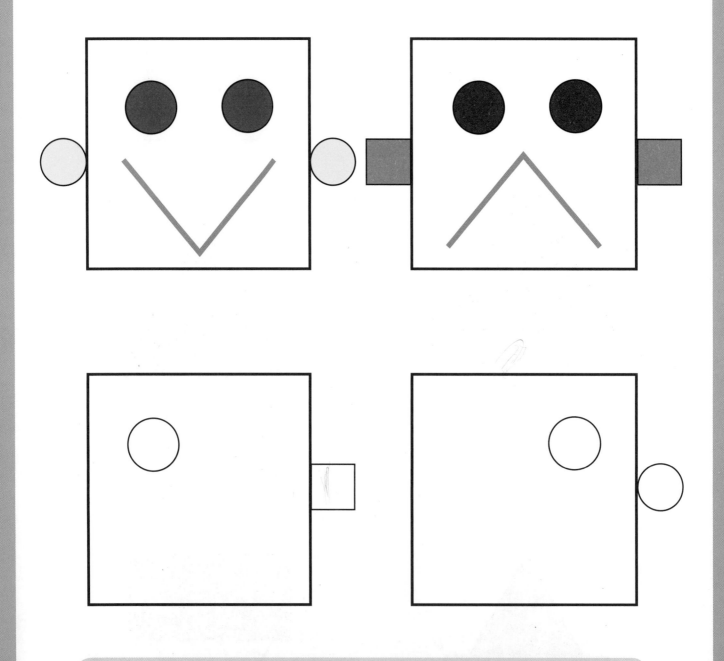

Color the pictures when you are finished drawing.

*For more activities like this, please see our *Thinker Doodles*™ series.

Find the figure that doesn't belong.
Then explain why it doesn't belong.

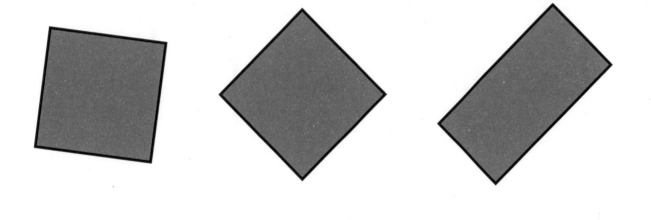

*Accept any answer that the student can logically defend.

I have four sides,
that are all the same.
My sides make four corners.
What is my name?

Of the four pictures that you see,
tell me now, can you find me?

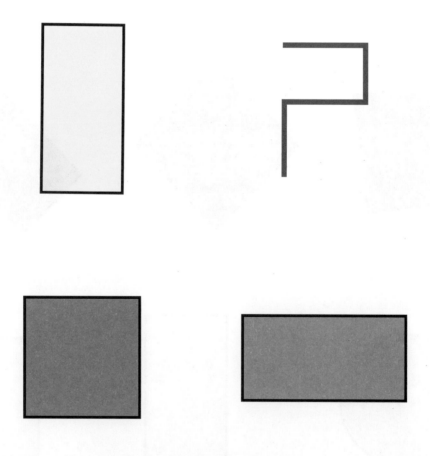

*For more activities like this, please see our *Can You Find Me?*™ series.

Which picture happened first?
Which picture happened next?
Which picture happened last?

The girl is behind her dad.

The boy is behind his mom.

Who is the boy behind?
Who is the girl behind?

Who is the cat behind?
Who is the dog behind?

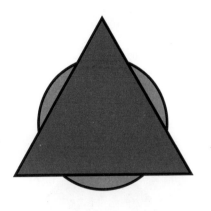 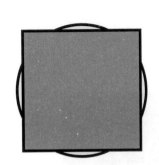 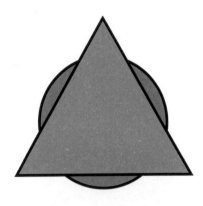

What is behind the blue triangle?

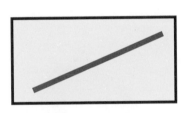  

What is behind the curved line?

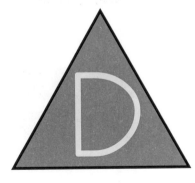  

What is behind the straight and curved line?

Which two figures are made with the same two shapes? What are the two shapes?

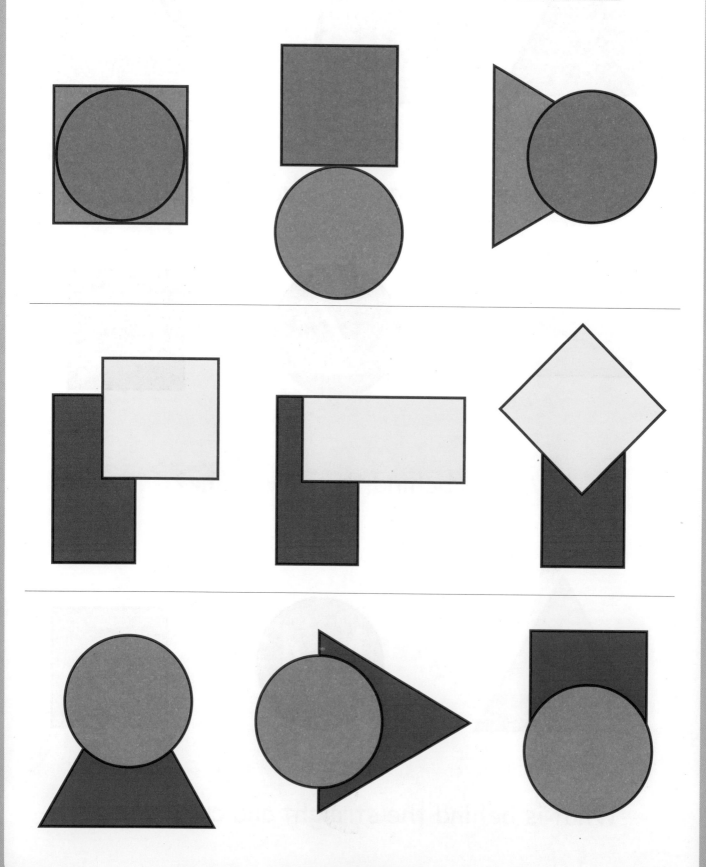

Which picture happened first?
Which picture happened next?
Which picture happened last?

Which two figures are made with the same two shapes? What are the two shapes?

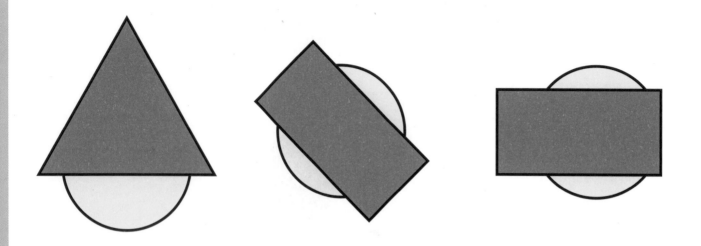

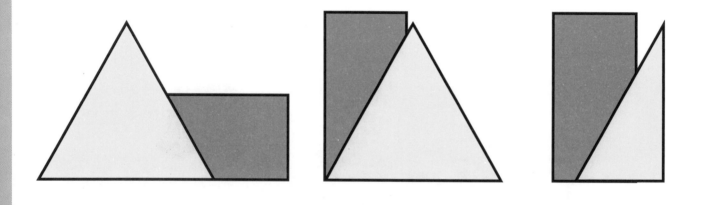

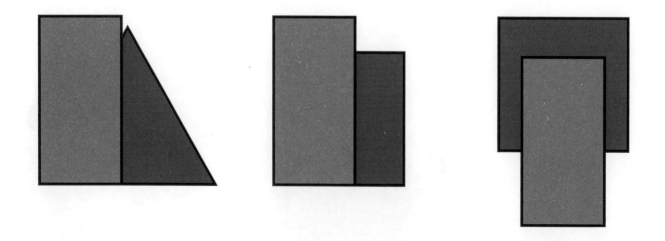

In which box does each figure below belong?
Draw a line from each figure to its box.

Which two figures are made with the same two shapes? What are the two shapes?

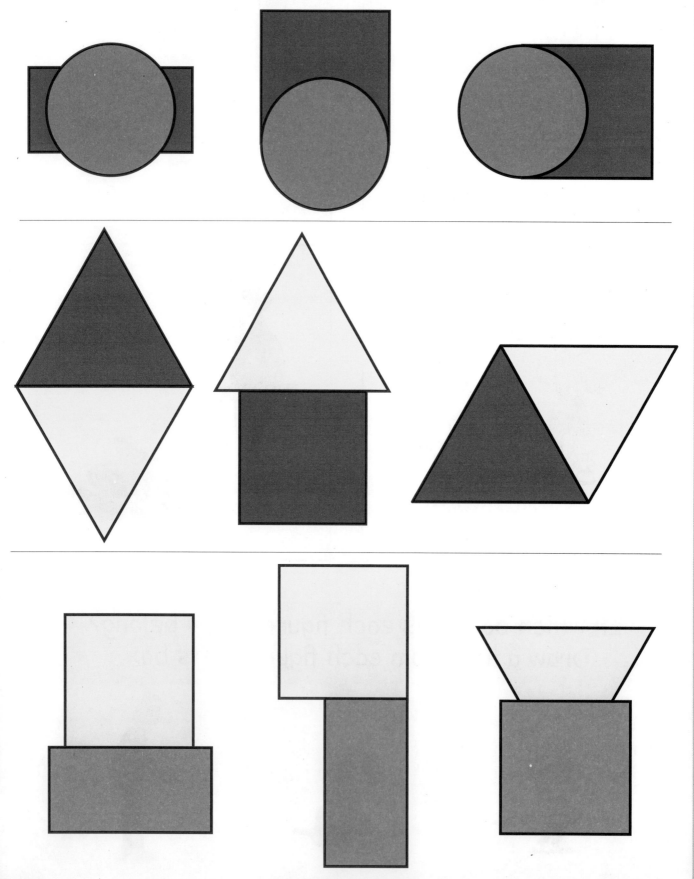

EFT

Which picture happened first?
Which picture happened next?
Which picture happened last?

What will happen to the snowman when the air outside starts to get warm?

FFT

The boy is shorter
than his mom.

The green line is shorter
than the red line.

Which color line is the shortest?

Which person is the shortest?

EFT

The blue snake is longer than the red snake.

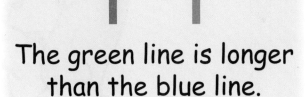

The green line is longer than the blue line.

Which color line is the longest?
Which color line is the shortest?

Which color line is the longest?
Which color line is the shortest?

Look at each figure below and find it in the picture.

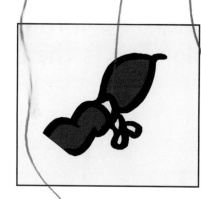

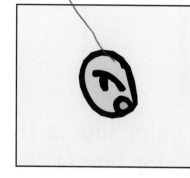

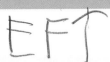

Which color rectangle is the shortest?

Which color rectangle is the longest?

Which color rope is the longest?

Which color rope is the shortest?

Which color string is the shortest?

Which color string is the longest?

Which color lines are shorter than the red line?

Which color line is the shortest line?

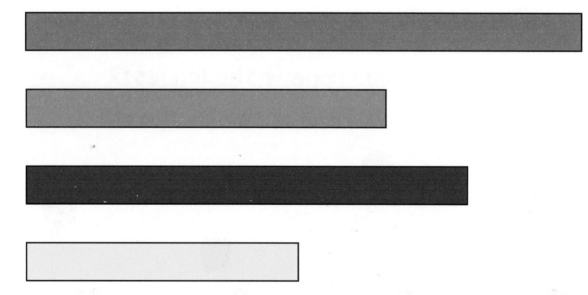

Which color rectangles are longer
than the blue rectangle?

Which color rectangle is the longest?

Point to the shortest green line.

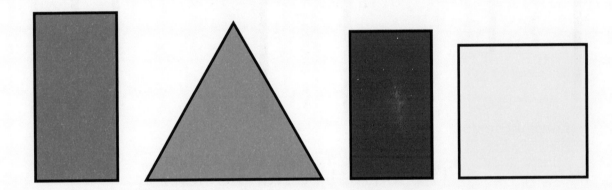

Point to the shortest rectangle.

*You might have to remind the student that a square is a type of rectangle.

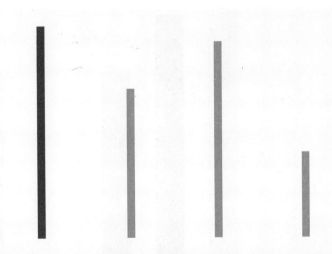

Point to the longest blue line.

Point to the group I describe.

The shortest line next to a red line

The longest rectangle next to a blue rectangle

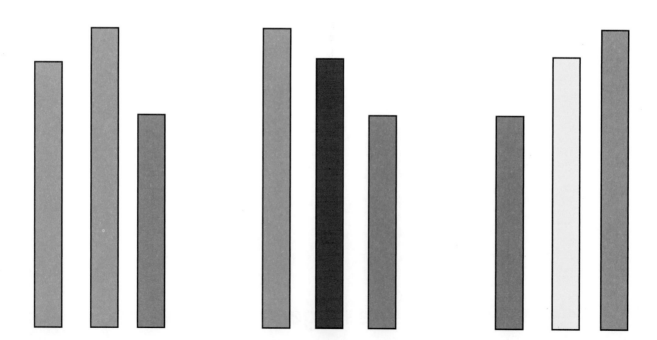

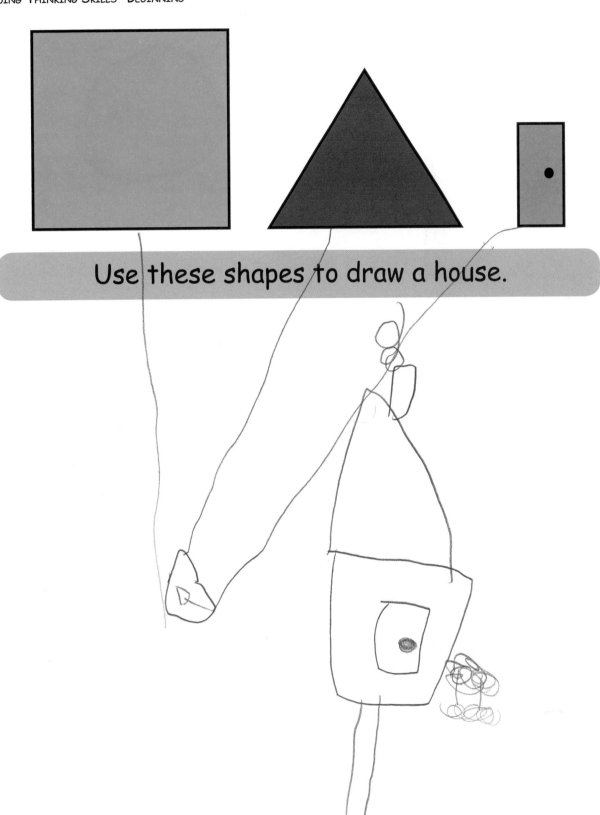

Use these shapes to draw a house.

What else can you add to your picture?

This is a whole cookie.

This is a half a cookie.

Point to the whole hot dog, then the half a hot dog.

 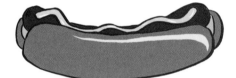

Point to the whole pizza, then the half pizza.

 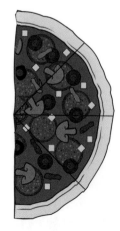  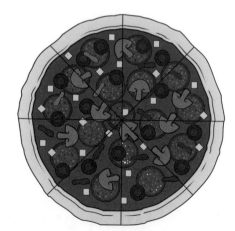

Point to and say whole glass, then half glass.

Point to and say whole footprint, then half footprint.

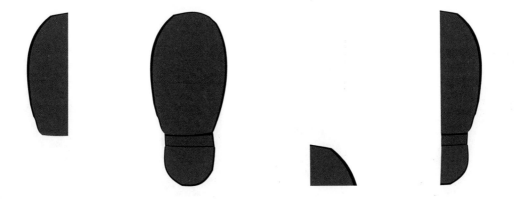

Point to and say whole apple, then half apple.

Point to the picture that is half of the whole figure.

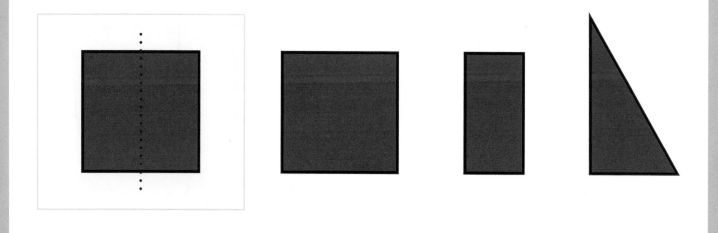

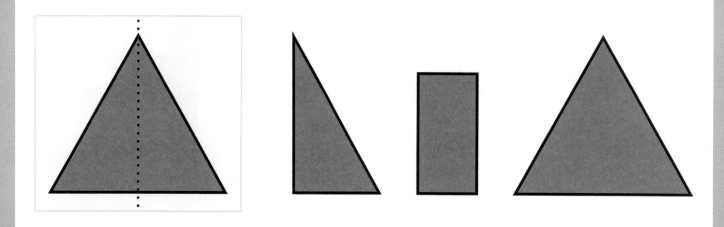

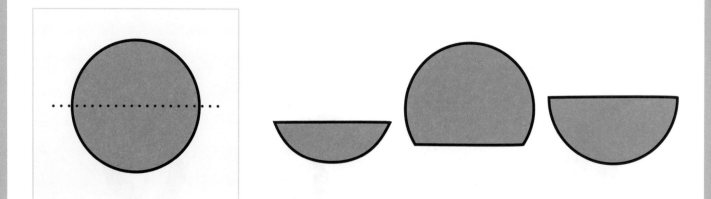

I'm not whole,
I'm just a part.
With two of me,
you'd have a full heart.

Of the four pictures that you see,
tell me now, can you find me?

*For more activities like this, please see our *Can You Find Me?*™ series.

Point to the picture that is half of the whole figure.

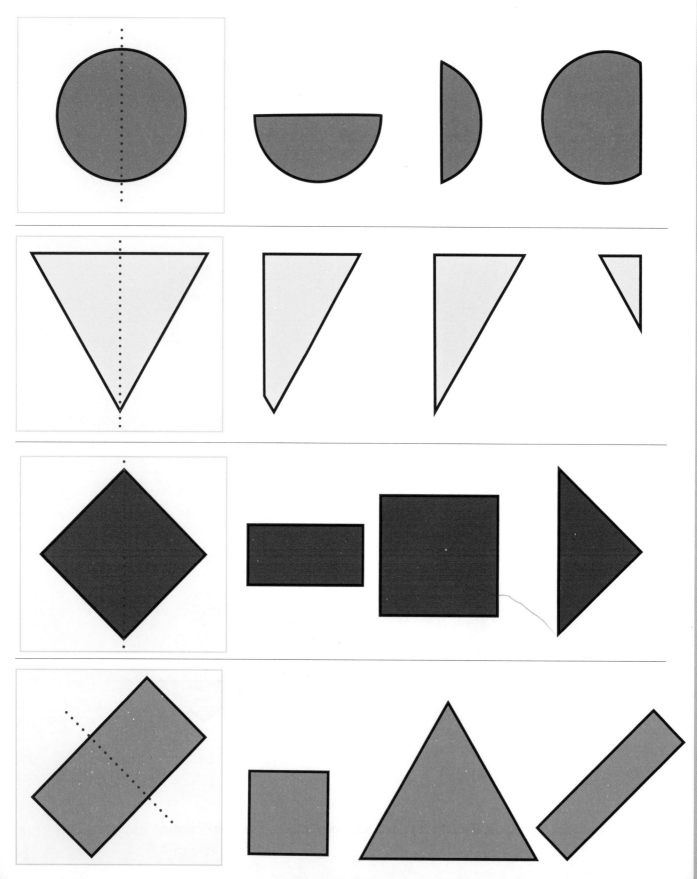

Point to the picture that is half of the whole figure.

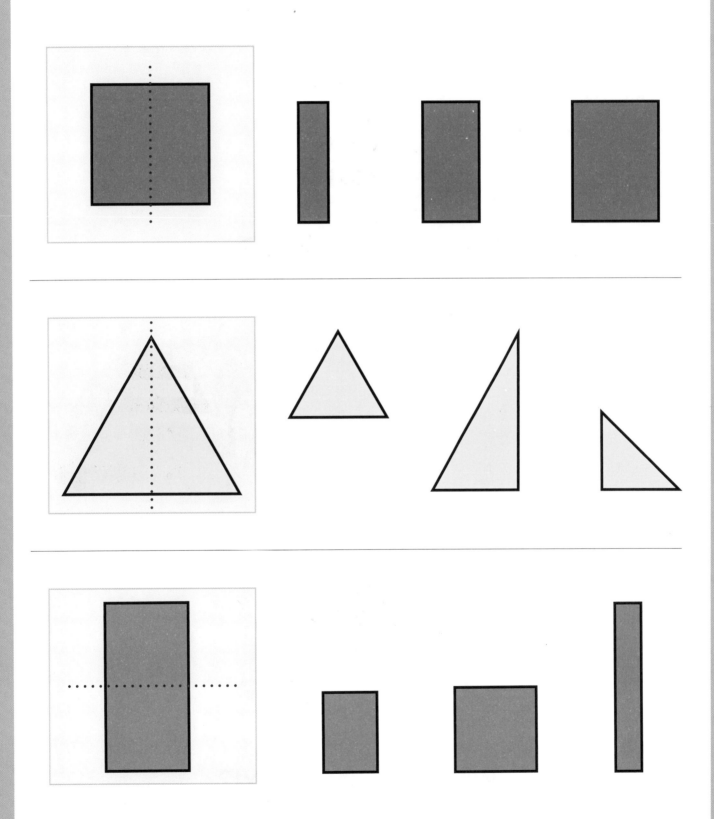

Which picture happened first?
Which picture happened next?
Which picture happened last?

What will happen next?

Bob ate half an apple,
he left the rest for Sue.
Sue ate half of what was left,
then left the rest for you.

Of the four pieces down below,
which is yours, do you know?

*If the student struggles with the problem, try demonstrating with a real apple.

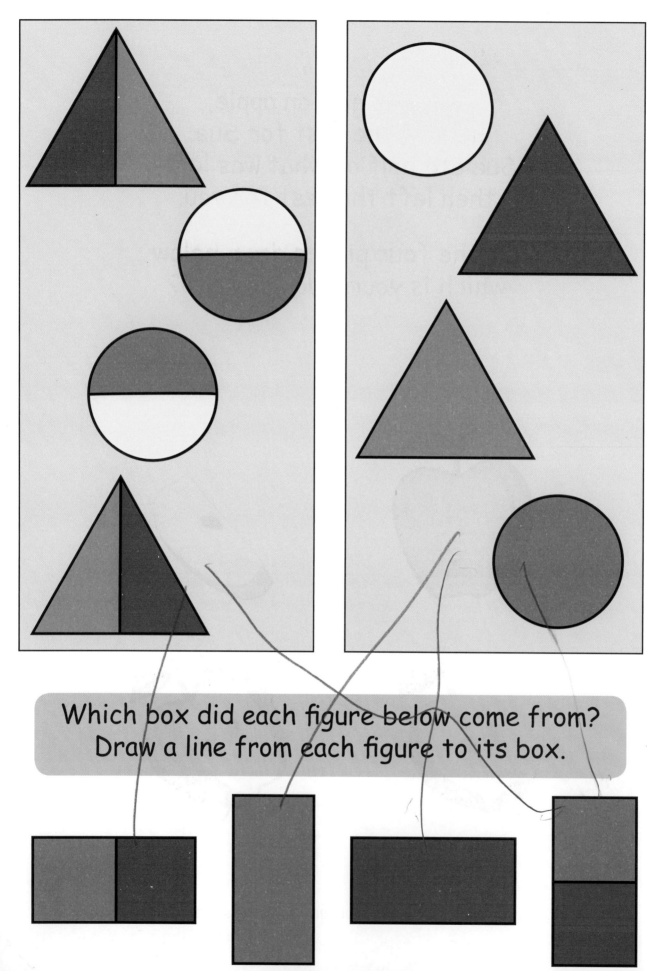

Which box did each figure below come from?
Draw a line from each figure to its box.

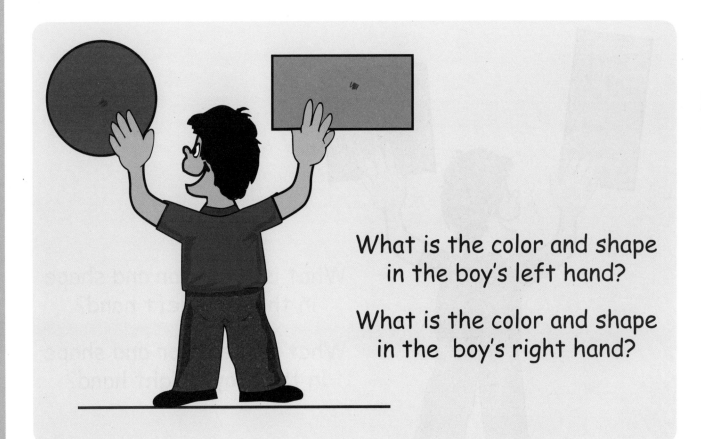

What is the color and shape in the boy's left hand?

What is the color and shape in the boy's right hand?

What is the color and shape
in the boy's right hand?

What is the color and shape
in the boy's left hand?

What is the color and shape
in the boy's left hand?

What is the color and shape
in the boy's right hand?

What color and shape is in the girl's right hand?

What color is the girl's left shoe?

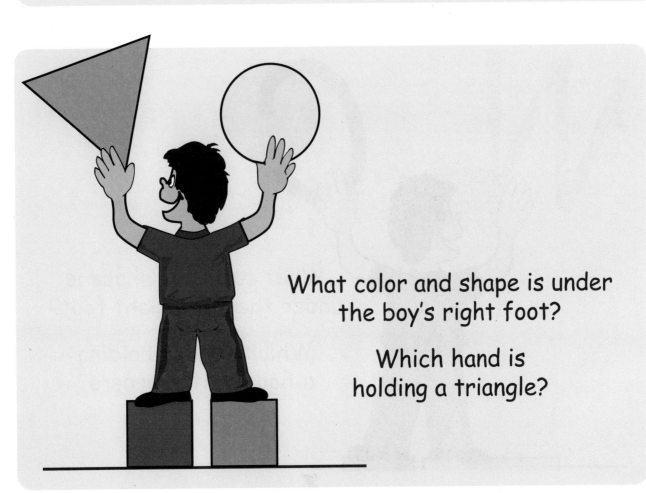

What color and shape is under the boy's right foot?

Which hand is holding a triangle?

EFT

What color and shape is under the girl's left foot?

Which hand is holding a straight and curved line?

What color and shape is under the boy's right foot?

Which hand is holding a figure with corners?

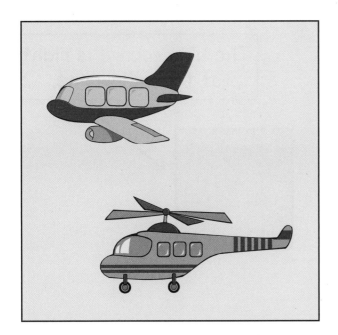

In which box does each figure below belong? Draw a line from each figure to its box.

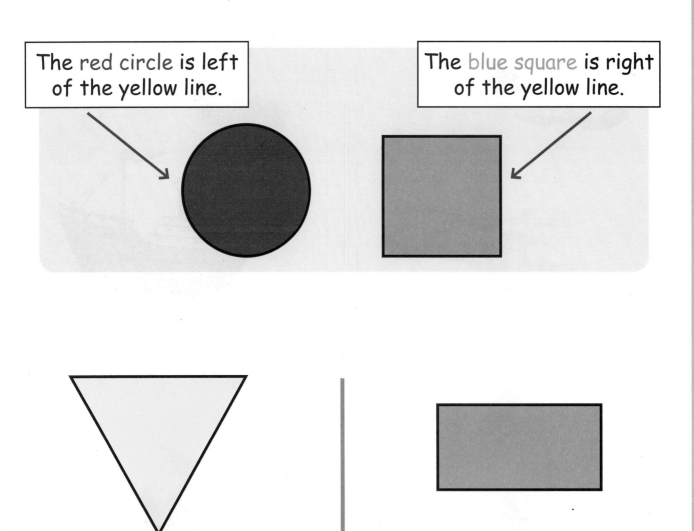

The red circle is left of the yellow line.

The blue square is right of the yellow line.

What is the color and shape of the figure on the left?

What is the color and shape of the figure on the right?

I am up above,
not down below.
I'm next to something,
small and slow.

Of the four pictures that you see,
tell me now, can you find me?

*For more activities like this, please see our *Can You Find Me?*™ series.

EFT

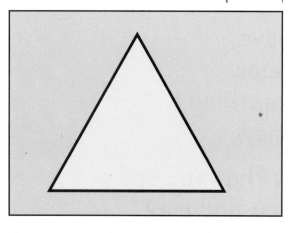 

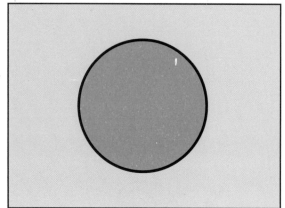 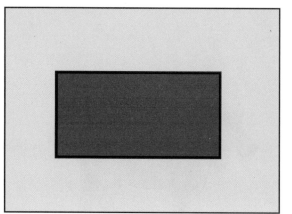

What is the color and shape of the figure on the bottom right?

What is the color and shape of the figure on the top left?

What is the color and shape of the figure on the top right?

What is the color and shape of the figure on the bottom left?

EFT

Answer straight, curved, or straight and curved.

What type of line is on the lower left?

What type of line is on the upper left?

What type of line is on the lower right?

What type of line is on the upper right?

Point to the group I describe.

A boy in between his best friend and her little sister

Something in between something smaller and larger

I'm on the left,
next to red on the right.
I hide all day,
and hunt all night.

Of the six animals that you see,
tell me now, can you find me?

*For more activities like this, please see our *Can You Find Me?*™ series.

Point to the figures I describe.

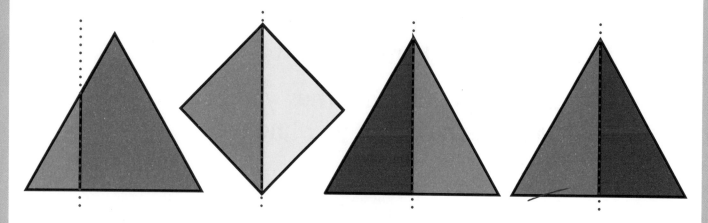

A triangle that is half blue

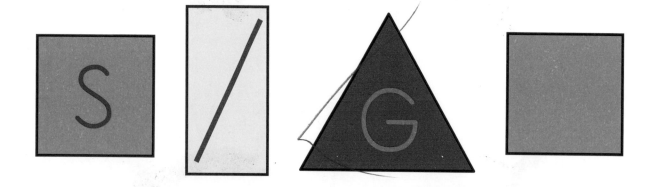

A square with a curved <u>or</u> straight line

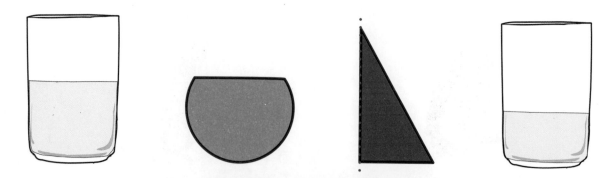

A half glass of water <u>or</u> a half circle

Find the path from the half glass to the half cookie.

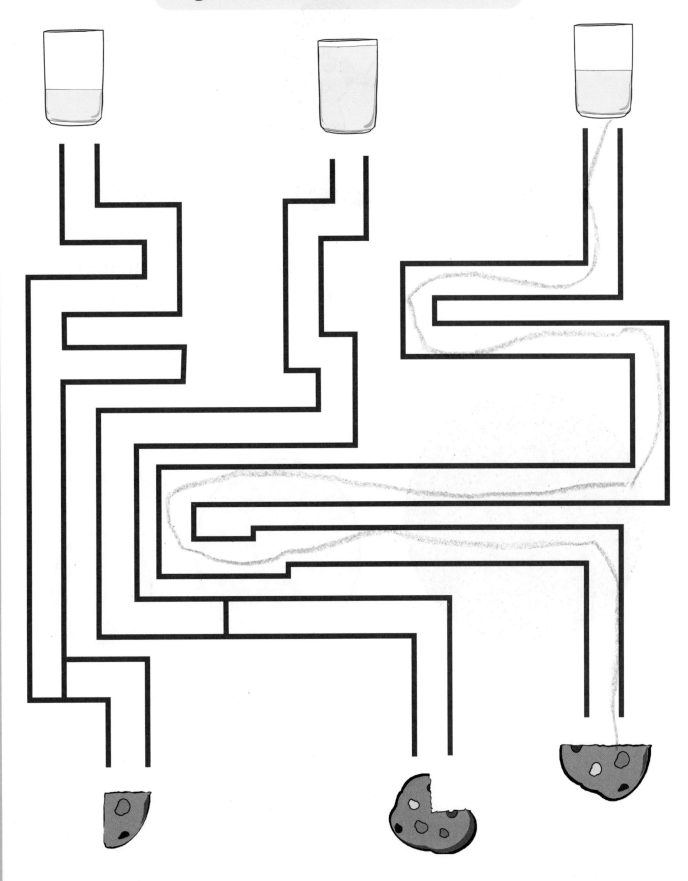

This man is
the largest.

This woman is
smaller than
the man.

This girl is
the smallest.

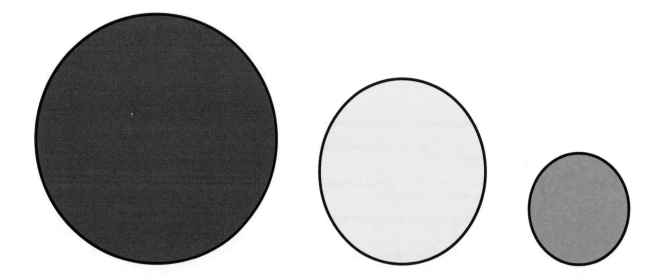

Which color circle is the largest?

Which color circle is smaller than the
largest but is not the smallest?

Which color circle is the smallest?

Say largest, smaller, and smallest as you point to the correct picture.

 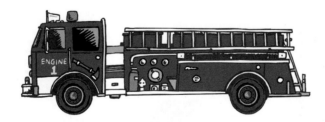 

Say largest, smaller, and smallest as you point to the correct picture.

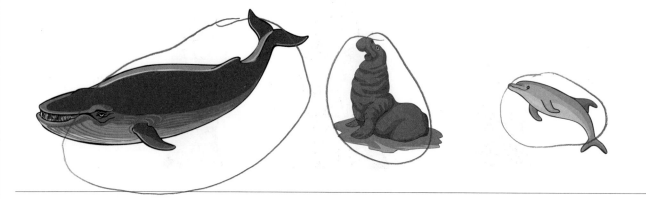

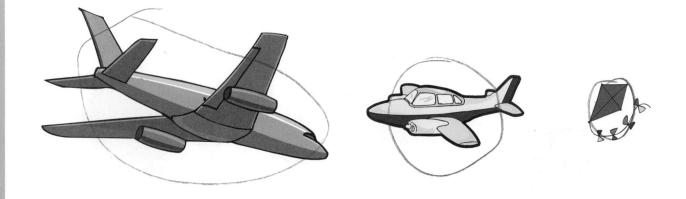

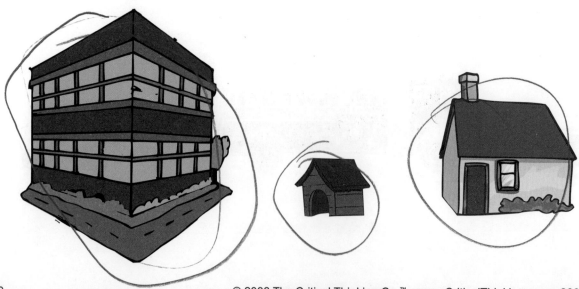

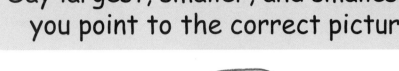

Say largest, smaller, and smallest as you point to the correct picture.

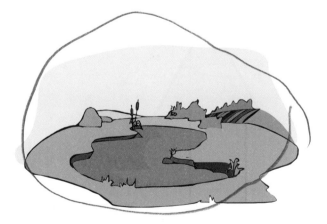

Say largest, smaller, and smallest as you point to the correct picture.

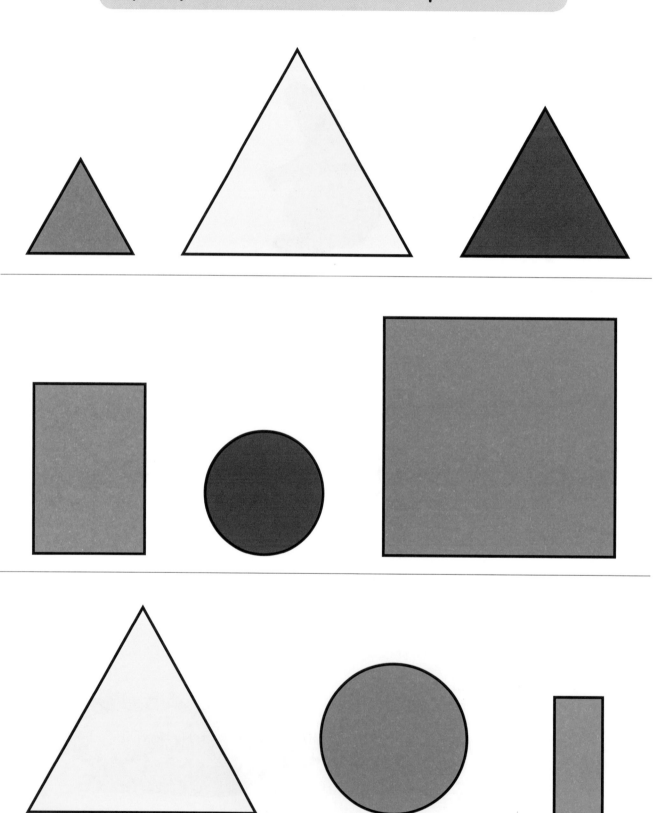

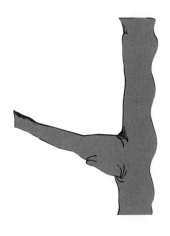 

Use each figure to draw a complete picture.

What else can you add to your drawing?
Are all the family members in the picture?

Point to the figure that I describe.

The smallest blue circle

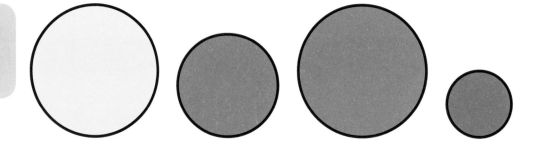

The smallest green curved line

6 9 Z s

The largest red rectangle

Point to the figure I describe.

A green
square next to
the smallest
red circle

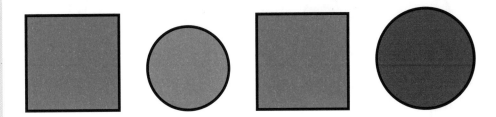

The straight
line next to a
yellow rectangle

The shortest
line next to a
green line

Which two figures are made with the same two shapes? What are the two shapes?

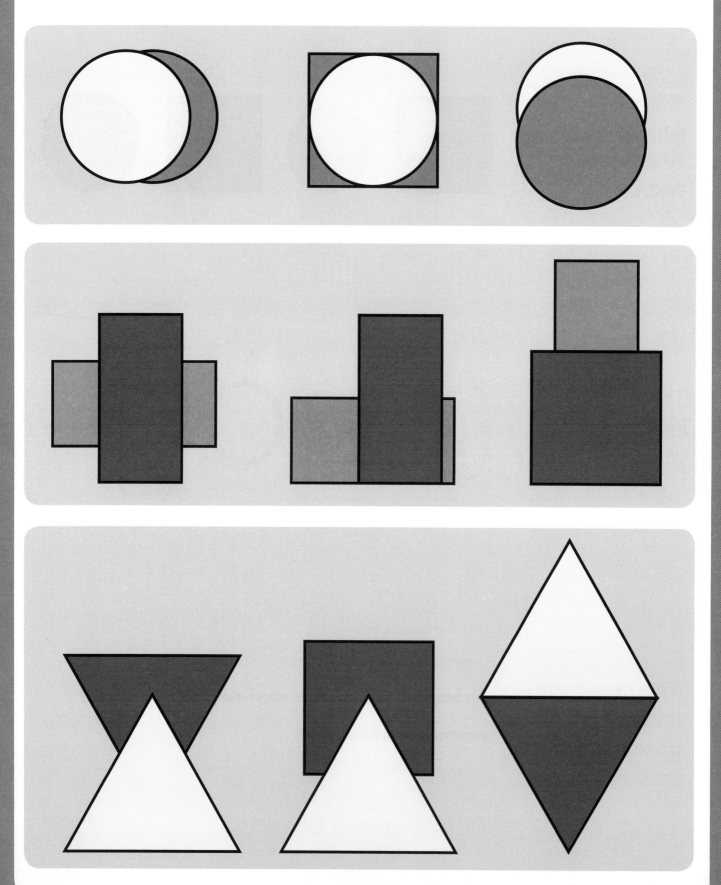

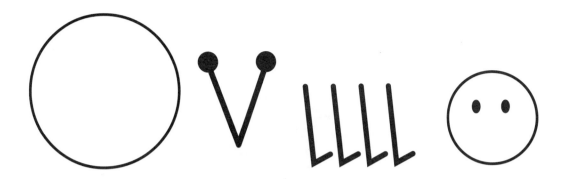

Use each of these parts to draw a bug.

What else can you add to the picture?
What does the bug eat?

EFT

Point to the group I describe.

A girl in between her younger brother and her pet

A bird above a boy and his mom

Circle the next picture in the pattern.

EFT

Complete the last picture in the pattern.

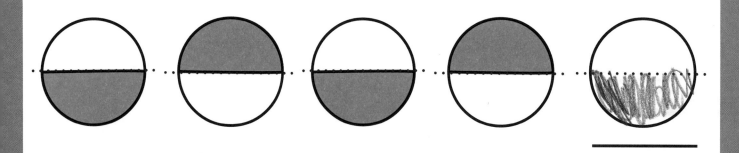

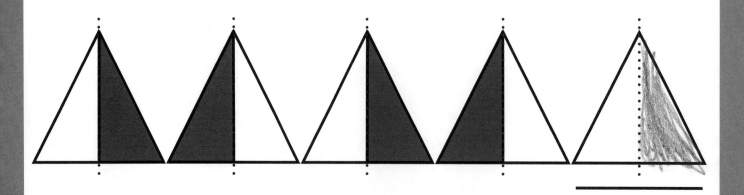

Sophia put her food in a row.
She made the pattern you see below.

Of the three foods that you see,
which food should the next one be?

*For more activities® like this, please see our *Can You Find Me?*™ series.

Circle the shape that comes next.

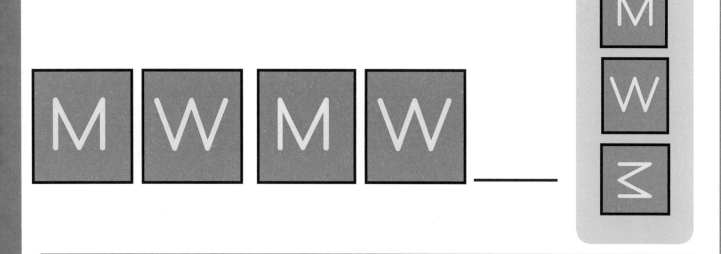

PFT

Look at each face above, then find its unfinished picture below. Use a pencil to draw in all the missing parts.

Color the pictures when you are finished drawing.

*For more activities like this, please see our *Thinker Doodles*™ series.

Find the figure that doesn't belong.

 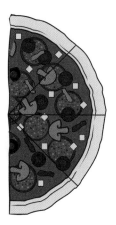 

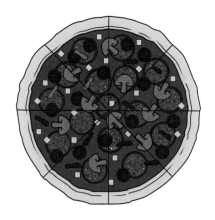  

*Accept any answer that the student can logically defend.

Point to the figure that I describe.

A red
triangle
behind the
largest bug

The
rectangle
behind the
smallest fly

*You may have to remind the student that a square is a special type of rectangle.

The largest
head behind
a figure
with three
corners

Smarty Pants Puzzle®

Tommy promised his mom he would clean his room before he went to sleep. He kept his promise.

Answer each question "yes" or "no."

1. If Tommy is dressed in his pajamas, he <u>must</u> have cleaned his room?

2. If Tommy is asleep, has he already cleaned his room?

3. If Tommy's room was messy when he fell asleep, someone messed it up after he cleaned it.

4. Tommy cleaned his room sometime before he went to sleep.

Answers: 1. No, 2. Yes, 3. Yes, 4. Yes.

* For more activities like this, please see our *Smarty Pants Puzzles®* series.

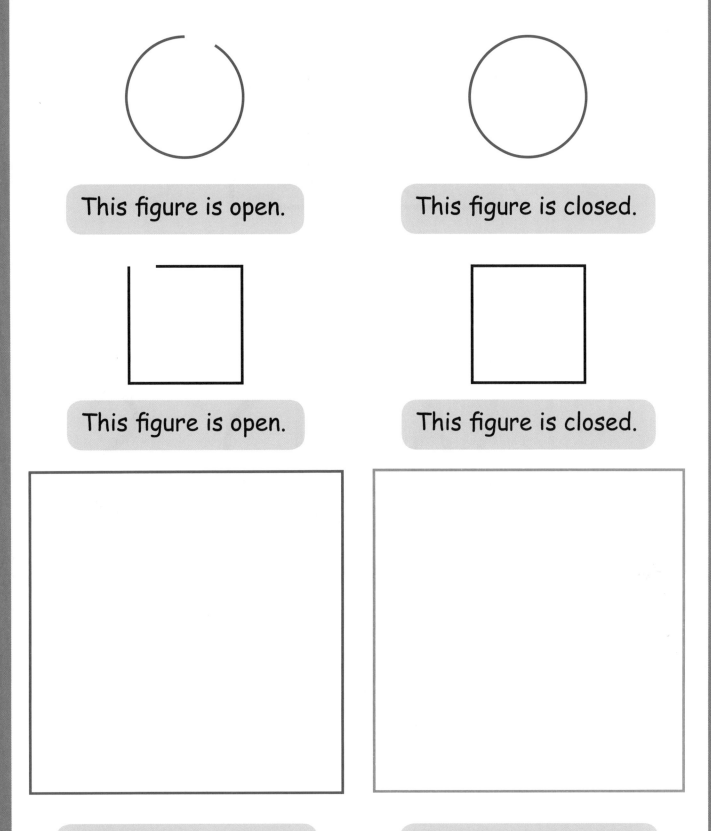

This figure is open.

This figure is closed.

This figure is open.

This figure is closed.

Draw an open figure
inside the red square.

Draw a closed figure
inside the blue square.

Point to the closed figures.

H W D S

Point to the open figure.

Draw an open figure
left of the line.

Draw a closed figure
right of the line.

Find the figure I describe.

An open figure next to a red figure

A closed figure next to a green triangle

An open figure left of a closed rectangle*

* A square is a rectangle.

Circle the next picture in the pattern.

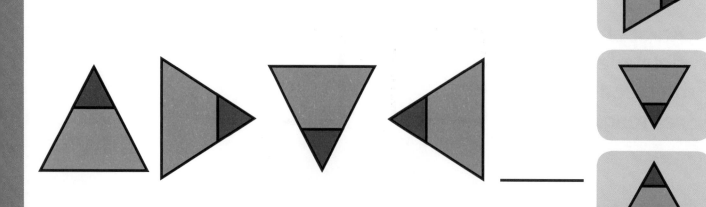

Which picture happened first?
Which picture happened next?
Which picture happened last?

What will happen next?

Circle the next picture in the pattern.

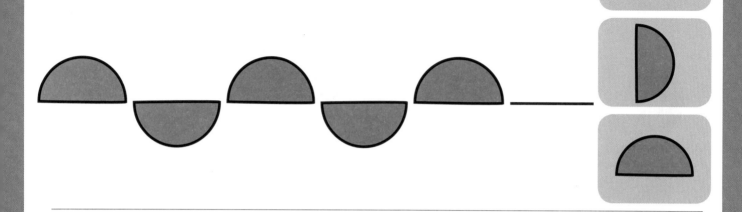

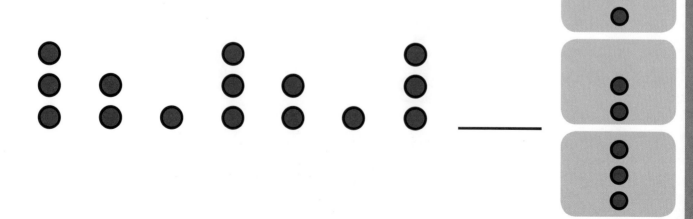

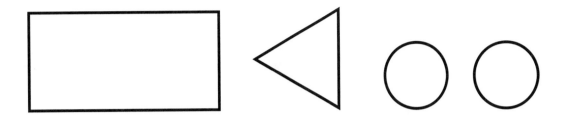

Use these shapes to draw a car.

What else can you add to your picture?
Is it raining or is the sun out?

Point to the line I describe.

G D O M

A line that is open and red

D B O Z

A line that is open or blue

◿ T S O

A line that is closed and made with straight lines

Point to the figure I describe.

ᕋ A C Z

A line that is curved <u>and</u> green _____

L X S T

A line that is curved <u>or</u> green _____

N S C ᕋ

A line that is blue <u>or</u> straight _____

B Y C W

A line that is straight <u>and</u> curved _____

Look at each pair of pictures.
They go together—can you see?

Now find the one that's missing.
Which picture should it be?

*For more activities like this, please see our *Can You Find Me?*™ series.

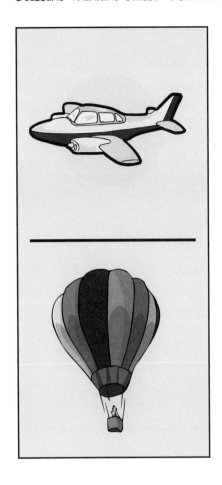

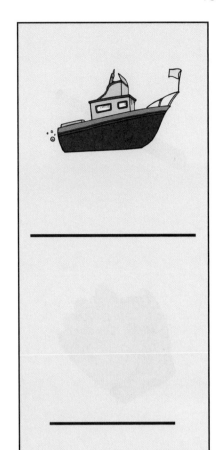

Look at each pair of pictures, there are always two of a kind.

See how they are alike, then you will know what to find.

*For more activities like this, please see our *Can You Find Me?*™ series.

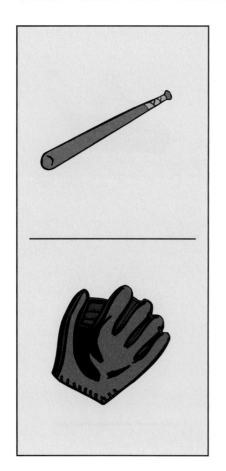

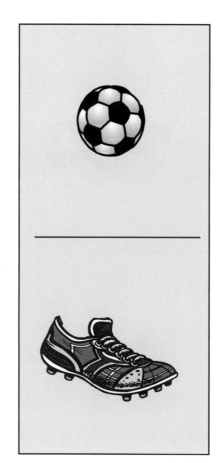

Look at each pair of pictures.
They go together—can you see?

Now find the one that's missing.
Which picture should it be?

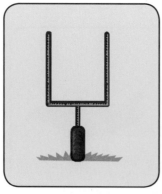

*For more activities like this, please see our *Can You Find Me?*™ series.

Look at each figure below
and find it in the picture.

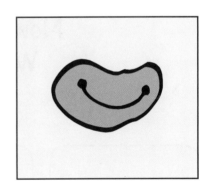

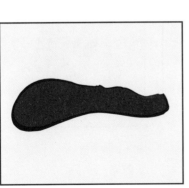

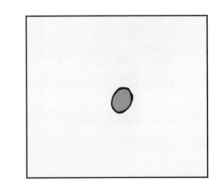

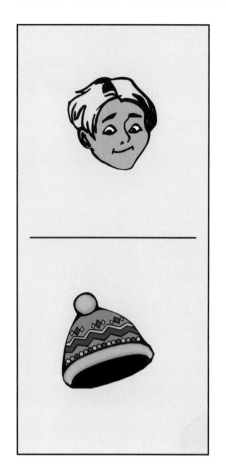

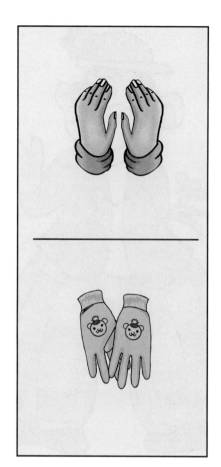

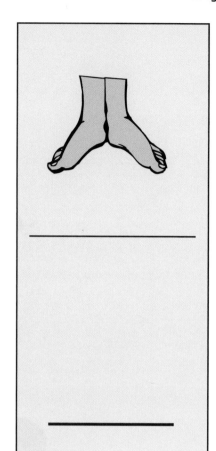

Look at each pair of pictures.
They go together—can you see?

Now find the one that's missing.
Which picture should it be?

*For more activities like this, please see our *Can You Find Me?*™ series.

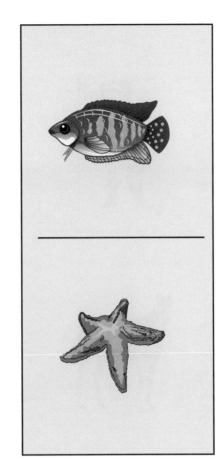

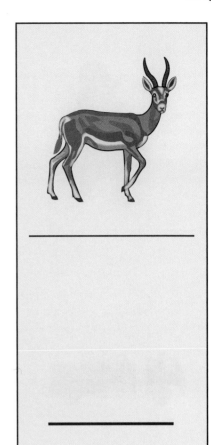

Look at each pair of pictures, there are always two of a kind.

See how they are alike, then you will know what to find.

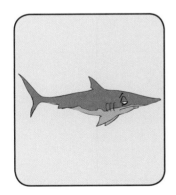

*For more activities like this, please see our *Can You Find Me?*™ series.

Look at each pair of pictures.
They go together—can you see?

Now find the one that's missing.
Which picture should it be?

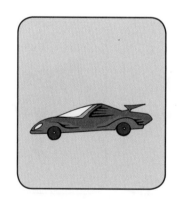

*For more activities like this, please see our *Can You Find Me?*™ series.

Look at each pair of pictures,
there are always two of a kind.

See how they are alike, then you
will know what to find.

*For more activities like this, please see our *Can You Find Me?*™ series.

Circle the missing picture.

* We do not try to define "analogy" for students because the definition is overwhelming for preschoolers. However, many students   grasp the concept after completing the activities on the next few pages.

Circle the missing picture.

 :  ::  : _____

 :: : _____

Circle the missing picture.

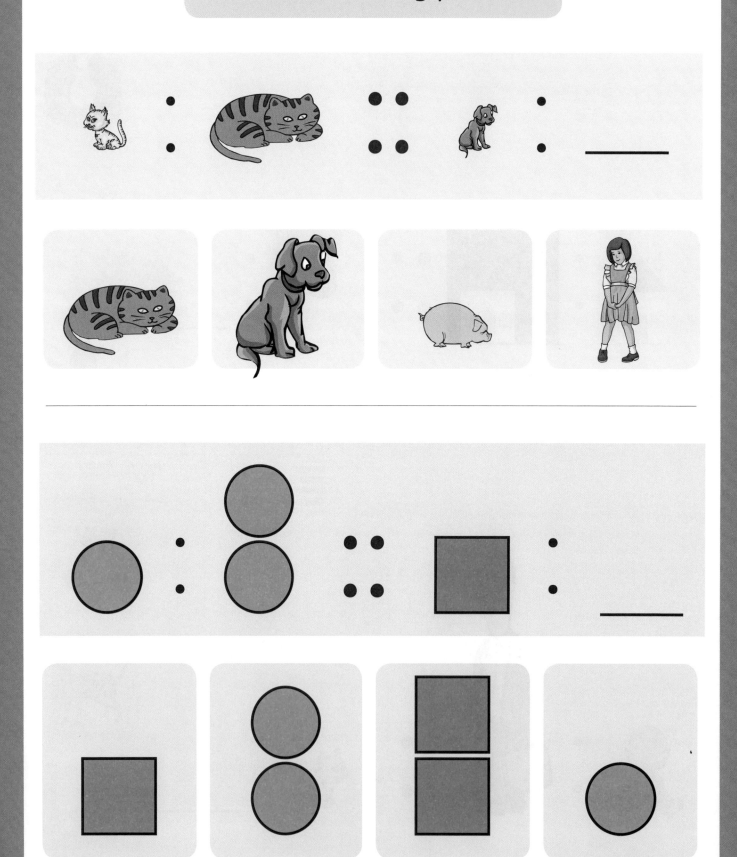

All of Tim's sisters have curly hair or two socks. Circle Tim's sisters.

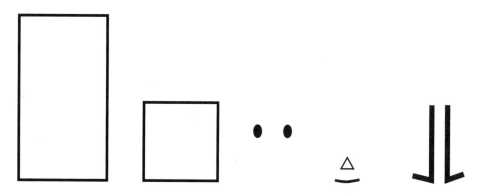

Use these shapes to draw a robot.

What else can you add to your picture?
Does the robot have a pet?

Circle the missing picture.

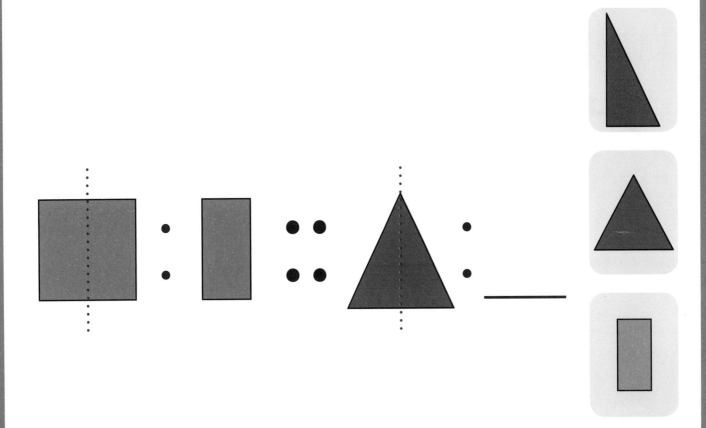

Circle the missing picture.

 :  : :  :  ____

 : 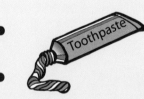 : :  :  ____

My picture has a triangle.
My picture has a square.
My picture has two circles,
and me with long brown hair.

Of the three pictures that you see,
which picture was made by me?

*For more activities like this, please see our *Can You Find Me?*™ series.

Circle the missing picture.

All of Marcia's figures are blue <u>or</u> have corners. Circle Marcia's figures.

Circle the missing picture.

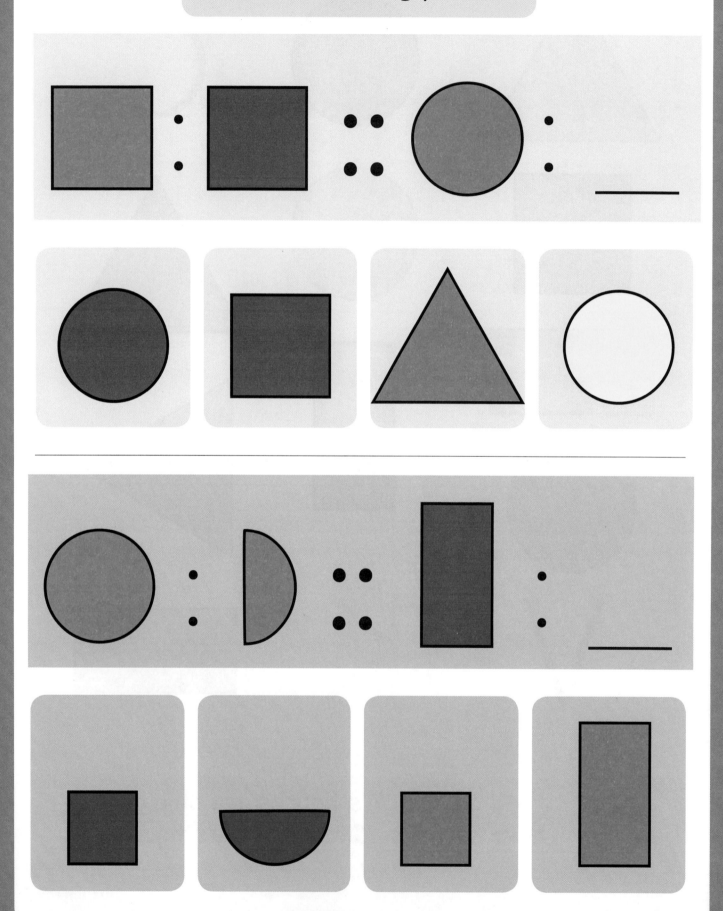

Circle the missing picture.

All of these go fast.
None is really slow.
Which two are faster?
Tell me if you know.

Of the four pictures that you see,
tell me now, can you find me?

*For more activities like this, please see our *Can You Find Me?*™ series.

Babe is the biggest.
I am the tallest.
Babe has four legs.
Max is the smallest.

Of the three animals that you see,
tell me now, can you find me?

*For more activities like this, please see our *Can You Find Me?*™ series.

Max is bigger.
Ben is smaller.
Max is shorter.
Ben is taller.

Max, Ben, and Bob are below.
Who is who, do you know?

*For more activities like this, please see our *Can You Find Me?*™ series.